Centaur Mon

CHIMNEY POTS AND STACKS

VALENTINE FLETCHER

CHIMNEY POTS
AND STACKS

An introduction to their
history, variety and identification

Foreword by
J. H. B. Peel

CENTAUR PRESS

ISBN 0 90000135 6

New material typeset by
Willow-Type, East Dean, Sussex PO18 0JB
Printed and bound by
Antony Rowe Ltd, Chippenham, Wiltshire SN14 6QA

CONTENTS

LIST OF PLATES

LIST OF FIGURES

PUBLISHER'S NOTE

So far as is known, this book is the first and only study concerned exclusively with chimney pots and stacks, and is therefore intended as an introduction rather than as a definitive work. Readers are invited to submit any information they may have concerning the design, dating, situation and makers' markings of any hand-made pots of which they have knowledge. Photographs or other illustrations will be most welcome. Such information will be of great assistance in the compiling of a fuller study at a later date.

PREFACE

The publication of this book in 1968 prompted a growing interest in chimney pots. Students of ceramics, vernacular architecture, and social history, have sought information historical, local and technical. Such manufacturers as remain have supplied such enquirers with catalogues and have given conducted tours of their factories. For example, Red Bank of Measham, Knowles of Elland, and Harris of Wrecclesham.

Although the ratio of cost to probable demand has prevented the publication of a much more exhaustive study, many photographic collections have been compiled and numerous conservationists and other devotees have made collections of the pots themselves. Prompted by this enthusiasm, Valentine Fletcher in 1978 assembled a museum of chimney pots. Between acquisition of a French "lighthouse" pot from Auxerre in 1978, and of a magnificent salt-glazed, louvred and horned pot were gathered. All Britain is represented, from Dorset to Caithness, and from Clwyd to Colchester, with additions from France, Italy and Portugal. Their close examination reveals details such as minute floral and geometrical bands of decoration and a wide range of makers' marks, including W. Rowe, Child Okeford; H. Doulton & Co., Rowley Regis (also Lambeth); C. Jennings, Poole; R. Spencer, Sturminster Newton; J. Oliver, Fareham; Hathern Pottery, Loughborough.

The Fletcher collection of chimney pots is displayed at the Park Farm Museum, Milton Abbas (near Blandford Forum), Dorset, which is visited by over 20,000 people each year. The museum is open from Mothering Sunday until the last Sunday of half-term in October. Details may be obtained by telephoning (0258) 880704.

ACKNOWLEDGEMENTS

The writer wishes to thank a number of people for help with this monograph. In the first place, he must express his indebtedness to the notes and papers of the late Mr. C. G. Dobson, who was to have written this book in the first place. He is grateful to Dr. Margaret Wood, for permission to quote from her book *The English Mediaeval House;* to Messrs. Batsford for permission to quote from A. Clifton Taylor's *Patterns of English Building;* to Messrs. Crosby Lockwood for permission to quote from R. Barry's *The Construction of Buildings;* to Messrs. Faber for permission to quote from H. Braun's *Old English Houses;* to Messrs. Longmans for permission to quote from W. B. MacKay's *Building Construction;* to the Technical Press Ltd. for permission to quote from P. L. Marks' *Chimneys and Flues;* and to the National Clayware Federation for permission to quote from E. W. Marchant's *Domestic Flues.*

He wishes to thank the National Clayware Federation for permission to reproduce matter from their catalogue; also *The Countryman* for permission to reproduce the photographs by Mr. G. T. Nicolle and the drawings of Provençal chimneys by Mr. R. H. Langbridge. He is grateful to the Bodleian Library, Oxford, and to the Oxford City Library and Reference Library, for their kind consideration and help; also to Miss Janet Flory, formerly Librarian of the University of Virginia.

He wishes to express his thanks to Mr. M. G. Alford, Mr. A. C. Cowan, Professor F. Celoria and Mr. G. T. Nicolle for photographing or arranging the photography of a number of chimneys; also to Mr. R. H. Langbridge for the use of his drawings and to Hugh E. Allen for some useful research notes.

He is most grateful to Mr. Jon Wynne-Tyson for much help and advice and kindly interest; and to his (the writer's) wife and son for bearing with a heavy load of caminology for many months, and for drawing his attention to a number of interesting chimneys in the flesh and in books; also for help with the proofs and the index.

FOREWORD

Most people either do not notice chimneys, or dismiss them as objects of no interest. Yet chimneys create a skyline of homely, human things . . . not seldom of beautiful things, for beauty does belong to the patterns carved by the chimneys of a Jacobean mansion.

This book opens our eyes to that beauty and to that homeliness. It tells us, for instance, that the Greeks had a word for chimney, *kapnodoke,* and that one of the purposes of a chimney is "to increase the velocity of ascent of the smoke by reducing the cross-sectional area of the outlet."

But this is something more than a general history of European chimneys. Despite his pastoral responsibilities in many parts of Britain, Mr. Fletcher has found time "to stand and stare" and then, like Captain Cuttle, to make a note of his observations. In Yorkshire he discovers "baked fireclay chimney-pots." In Suffolk he sees "stacks without any pots." In the Western Isles of Scotland he finds "a pot stuck in the thatch to serve as a chimney." The result offers glimpses into craftsmanship, geology, architecture, industry, French painting, and the hazards of chimney sweepers long ago.

J. H. B. Peel

Chapter One

INTRODUCTION

"Coo, what a sight!" exclaims the chimney-sweep in 'Mary Poppins' as from the rooftops he surveys the vast and variegated chimneyscape of London. Chimneys and chimneypots also play no small part in the popular saga of Father Christmas.

Yet chimney stacks and pots are a feature of the landscape we all take for granted, hardly notice, seldom speak about, never write about. This is strange, for they can become—like wallpaper patterns—an inevitable subject for meditation to such people as the prisoner, the hospitalized, and the sick at home, whose eyes are perforce glued upon them. They can become subjects for meditation to those who see them from offices or studies. One clergyman of my acquaintance relates how, from his study in Middlesborough nearly half a century ago, he would look out intently on the chimney-pots of the school which was named after the father of Gertrude Bell.

For my own part, ever since I was two years old I have been fascinated by chimneys and chimneypots. When I had been thus intrigued for half a century I ventured to write an article "In Praise of Chimney Pots" in a well-known periodical. I complained that no one had yet written a monograph on this subject. One could find the occasional reference in books on architecture or social history, but there was no monograph. What a thrill it was when I received a letter from a publisher who had read my article, asking me if I would write a book on Chimney Pots and Stacks.

During the research which has followed this invitation, my knowledge of chimneys has greatly increased, and the fascination continues unabated. No one could, however, be expected to go all round the world chimney-spotting, or all round Great Britain for that matter; no one could be expected to look at every book or every painting that may contain a reference to, or representation of, a chimney; so the scope for further study of the subject remains illimitable. Every time I travel any distance I see something remarkable in the way of a chimney-stack or pot: something new and strange. But what of driving without due care and attention? What of crowded roads, clearways and parking difficulties? So many chimneys of interest must go unrecorded and unnoticed.

Tennyson asked:

> Why the life goes when the blood is spilt?
> What the life is? where the soul may lie?
> Why the church is with a steeple built,
> And the house with a chimney-pot?
> Who will riddle one the how and the what?
> Who will riddle one the what and the why?

Tennyson put the chimney-pot in good company. It is almost true to say that, as the spire is to a church, so is the chimney to a house. Or is the chimney and its pots analogous to the head and face of a body—the roof providing the shoulders? It all depends on how you look at a building. Some are sufficiently chimney-conscious to name their houses 'High Chimneys', 'Three Chimneys', 'Red Chimneys' and so on. But most people never look at chimney-pots at all, and not so many look at chimneys. They may perhaps look at the chimneys of Compton Wynyates or of Chambord. But what of the ordinary, humble, chimneys and chimney-pots?

Where would a typical English townscape be without the skyline of chimneys and chimney-pots? Look over London from a high office desk, and see the almost symmetrical rows of many-potted stacks which surmount street after street. Look down a humble street in a northern industrial town, and see the long rows of identical houses, each having a little stack on the street side of the roof crowned by two 'Bishops', each stack like a dog's ear cocked up. Consider the mellowed and many-coloured variety of chimneys keeping guard over an old Cathedral city, the intensely variegated assortment that surmounts the houses and shops of a country market-place : the irregular display that beautifies the closely built village-street. What of the Elizabethan manor house? What of the stately Georgian townhouse? What of the English farmhouse and the country cottage? Remove the chimneys and their pots, and how much the poorer they would be, and in many cases how pedestrian they would become.

But the sad fact is, our British chimneys and chimney-pots are vanishing. Makers tell me that many handsome varieties of pots, which are artistic if not antique, are no longer being made. Others are considered obsolete. The chimney-pot, as we shall see later, is being debunked, and modern flues and flue-terminals substituted. Demolition squads at work on old properties—where the largest proportion of antique and interesting chimney-pots are to be found—could not care less about their preservation : they are the first things to be thrown to the ground and smashed. I once requested the preservation of a fine Victorian angel from the

gable of an old vicarage being demolished. Could I get it?
No; it was too costly of time and money to lower it carefully, so it 'got damaged'. If such was the fate of an angel,
can we hope for a better fate for chimney-pots? Worst of
all, from the point of view of a chimney-enthusiast, we
are going all-electric, and making many ancient and well-
chimneyed buildings all-electric too. The result is that,
to quote two examples, there is an old Berkshire town where
one side of the market place has been completely and
uniformly divested of its chimneys; and an old Sussex
Georgian inn which formerly stood proudly erect with four
fine gable chimneys (each bearing handsome pots), which
now looks like a trunk without a head. Moreover, in too
many new towns, housing areas, and private builders'
estates, chimneys are either non-existent or reduced to
the bare minimum—and the bare minimum of interest.

Britain has led the world in beautiful chimneys, and
intriguing assortments of pots—pots intriguing in themselves
and in their arrangement and effect. In this book I have
tried to trace the history of the chimney, then the development of the chimney-pot from its mediaeval use in England,
through several centuries of disuse, to its triumphant re-
appearance in the eighteenth century.

I have tried to list as many kinds of chimney-pot as
possible, together with their variations however slight. I have
remarked on the odd, interesting, and sometimes beautiful
effect of the various arrangements, permutations and combinations of chimney-pots; and on the various cowls which
often surmount the pot.

I have next noted the prevailing regional styles of chimneys and chimney-pots in Britain. Perhaps this is the most
fascinating subject of all. It is not easy to account for
these variations. I felt myself stumped for an answer

when a young lady from 'The Times' asked me on the 'phone what I considered might account for these regional varieties. It is not easy to answer such a question. It is possible to say that in the Lake District, for example, it was the choice of materials—slates and stones—which accounts for its almost unique chimney-devices. But the same Lake District also has its special preferences in the matter of actual chimney-pots. I suppose the real answer lies in what the nearest ceramics factories chose to turn out. Whatever accounts for them, regional variations there are in Britain; and in France too. But so far as Britain is concerned, you may blindfold me, put me in a plane, and set me down arbitrarily in any spot; take off the bandage, and I will tell you what region we are in by a look at the nearest vernacular chimneys or chimney-pots.

I spoke of France just now: for we must not imagine Britain to be the only country which has chimneys and chimney-pots, though to my mind it has the best and finest. I have tried to collect evidence as to the early use of chimneys and chimney-pots in other countries and as to the prevailing types of them in other lands today.

All this has made the study of this subject quite a detailed one. But it could have been much more so. There is much which I have not done, many interesting chimney-centres I could not visit. There are bound to be missing links in my historical findings. The scope remains endless, as the fascination remains endless. The contribution made by this present book can hardly be other than introductory.

B

Chapter Two

THE HISTORY OF THE CHIMNEY

In the American Revised Standard version of the Bible "the smoke out of the chimney" (Hosea 13, 3) has become "the smoke out of a window". We shall, however, find parallels in mediaeval times to the psalmists' "bottle in the smoke". To the Greeks, kaminos meant an oven or furnace; Galen used the word as meaning a flue; but further back, Herodotus (8, 137) used the word Kapnodoke in such a was as to leave us doubting whether he meant an opening in the roof or a chimney. Certainly in later Basilican Greek Kapnouchos meant a chimney. The Latin caminus meant principally a forge or oven or fireplace. We can remember the caminus which smoked poor Horace out on his way to Brundisium. It seems certain now that Greek houses had chimneys, if only in the kitchen, and that these chimneys were of wood. At Tiryns Schliemann said that the smoke found its outlet through the opening of a central dome. The Romans had elaborate vent and chimney systems, and though in many buildings the smoke escaped through doors, windows, and openings in the roof, yet chimneys were not unknown. After the Roman period, Britain returned to the open fire or hearth; though the use of central or gable-end smoke holes, vents, and louvres, stems from the use in prehistoric huts in northern lands.

According to the *Oxford Dictionary,* a chimney is the passage or flue by which the smoke of a fire ascends, or

(Middle English) the part which rises above the roof. The whole chimney is intended "to induce and maintain a draught providing a supply of fresh air to the fire. It will also act as a ventilator facilitating the change of air in a room." (*Encyclopaedia Britannica.*)

E. W. Marchant in *Domestic Flues* (National Clayware Federation, 1966) says "the function of the fabric of the chimney is to protect the flue from rapid changes in external environment, and to provide adequate structural strength to the flue for the whole of its length."

The word chimney in English originally meant a fireplace, and no date can be assigned to its first use in the modern sense. Other early English words were fumeral or femerel (1407 and later), tuel (1307: "vulgarly called chymnes" at York in 1364), and louvre or louver (1440: v. infra). Chaucer speaks of the "chemineys" of Vesuvius; and Shakespeare (by whose time there were plenty of chimneys) of "our chimneys" being "blown down" (*Macbeth*, 2, 3, 60). A chimney-shaft or chimney-stalk is the part of a chimney which rises above the roof top; or a tall mill or factory chimney. A chimney stack meant originally a group of chimney-stalks; we shall see how the modern chimney-stack evolved from this. A chimney-pot is a cylindrical pipe of earthenware or sheet-metal, fitted on the top of a chimney-shaft. In Scotland the pot is called a 'can'; a house in East Lothian was spoken of in 1895 as having 'fourteen chimley-cans', In parts of South-West England the word 'tun' replaces 'pot' or 'can'; "on the great chimney-tuns, as the country-folk call them, tribes of birds have taken up their residence" wrote Richard Jefferies in 1875.

Chimneys in 'Norman' times were confined to castles and very large houses. In ordinary houses there was no funnel of escape. In castles flues. were built into the walls, and the earliest type of Norman chimney can be found in early 12th century keeps: it was an oblong vent inside a shallow buttress. Castle Hedingham (1130) has, in the southern buttress, flues for fireplaces at two levels: a similar arrangement can be seen at Rochester. "The presence of two vents, one each side of a flat buttress, would enable the windowed vent to be closed in heavy weather, the leeward one being thus assisted, through the protection of the buttress, to draw more efficiently" (M. Wood, *The English Mediaeval House*). In the keeps of Tretower (Breconshire) and Ogmore (Glamorgan), circular draught holes run obliquely through back walls. At Portchester in Hants (1160-72) the north fireplace on the first floor has a flue going ten feet up the wall to a domed vault: narrow slits in the wall let out the smoke: something similar can be seen at Castle Rising and at Canterbury. By the middle of the twelfth century cylindrical chimneys had come in. They may have been common in stone houses. Framlingham Castle has two in the hall block, with lancet vents. Sometimes these chimneys do not reach ground level. Two types occur; one with an open top, and the other with side vents. There is a twelfth-century chimney extant at Puy-en-Velay in France, with a lantern of six trefoil headed openings, ungabled, beneath an elegant cone and finial. We shall meet others of this type of later date.

Outstanding examples of twelfth-century chimneys still extant are to be found at Christchurch Castle, Hants (here is the only extant Norman fireplace with a circular chimney); Boothby Pagnell Hall, Lincolnshire, similar, but with a gabled buttress; 79½ High Street, Southampton, removed from this site after bombing and reset in St. John's House; and a chimney dating from c. 1130 from Old Sarum, now reassembled in the Salisbury museum, with dog tooth moulding round its base. On the whole, twelfth-century chimney shafts were either cylindrical with an open top, or cylindrical with side vents and conical capping.

No chimneys appear on the Bayeux tapestry, though the manor house of Bosham as depicted thereon shows a most elaborate roof-finial, which some might be excused for interpreting as a chimney.

Thirteenth-century chimneys which can be dated include the magnificent gabled stack with lancet openings at Abingdon Abbey (plate 1) (c. 1260), chimneys at Aydon Castle (c. 1280), and Stokesay Castle (two pairs; c. 1285-1305), and a spired chimney on a house at Woodstock (c. 1290). Chimneys similar to this last-named are to be found on houses at Kingham, Oxfordshire (plate 3); Bredon, Worcestershire; and Motcombe, Dorset; all of the late thirteenth century. That at Kingham, which has been rebuilt, is round, has a ridge-tile, and is equipped with trefoil headed vents; it has a course, above which are gables, and the whole is surmounted by a conical top. On the whole, in the thirteenth century round capped chimneys gave way to polygonal chimneys, which were more convenient for 'window' arrangement. Examples of these are at Bredon, Woodstock, Motcombe (capped by a fleur de lys) and St. Briavel's Castle in Monmouthshire (capped by a constable's horn). But open cylindrical chimneys were still fashionable and were used in royal castles, as at Criccieth and Conway. The most remarkable thirteenth-century chimneys extant are probably those at Abingdon, St. Lo in Normandy, and Bayeux. That at Abingdon is oblong with four gables; on the east side is one oblong opening, on the other sides three lancets each; a larger arch behind these openings gives on to the flue. Below it is a

magnificent stone-canopied fireplace, the canopy of which
was supported by shafts (now missing) and beautifully carved
foliated capitals. To the north of it is an interior chimney
from a fireplace made in the crypt to heat the wine stored
there : from this chimney the smoke escapes by an opening
in the wall protected by two vertical stones secured by
corbels (plate 1). That at St. Lo is octagonal, has eight
arches, surmounted by sixteen arches, all topped by a
ribbed pyramidal spire. 'La Lanterne des Morts' at Bayeux,
just south-west of the Cathedral, is tall and cylindrical (plate
2); above a course, are sixteen lancet-shaped arches; in
the tapering cap are ten rows of smoke-holes. This chimney
got its name from the local legend that at the death of
any citizen of Bayeux a light was shown from it.

The conical chimneys of England and France shared a
common origin. They differed in that France substituted a
continuous arcade for the gabled windows of the English
chimneys.

From the thirteenth century the only other curiosity I
have been able to unearth is the ancient chimney and fireplace in the Manor House at Charney Bassett near Wantage,
which has a small oven to the right above the fireplace, for
baking the Sacramental Bread (the house has an ancient
thirteenth-century chapel).

It has been conjectured that chimneys were invented in
Italy, and that there were 'smokejacks' in Germany before
1350. There are chimneys in Gerard David's *Adoration of
the Shepherds* (early 14th century), and in *Good Government*
by Ambrozio Lorenzetti (1338-40) plenty of chimneys appear
in the town, some of these more like louvres than chimneys.
Fourteenth-century chimneys are commoner in Britain and Dr.
Margaret Wood (op. cit.) quotes twenty examples as extant.

At Carisbrooke in 1353 masons were employed to cut

freestone for a reredos in the kitchen, and to make above it
a wall of stone for fear of the fire (pro dubio foci) because
the wall that had been there was of lattice-work. Fourteenth-
century London ordinances compelled chimneys to be no
longer of wood, but of stone, tiles, or plaster. In 1317 the
Earl of Richmond's hall in London was to have the tewels
plastered to the top. In 1368 at Shene pipes were made
for the fireplaces of Edward III's palace with plaster of
Paris: four pipes for two presumably back to back fireplaces.
In the same year at Clipstone payment was made for
making two chimneys (caminorum) with plaster of Paris,
to replace two blown down by the wind. We hear of
eighteen shops in London whose chimneys had to be built,
in 1370, to rise one foot above the roof; earlier, in 1321, at
Hamsey Manor near Lewes, the chimneys had to rise
three feet above the roof. At Hadleigh (Essex) in 1363,
four earthen pots (olla lutea) were bought for the fumerell
of the barn, and four others for the smoke vent of the
King's hall in Rayleigh Park: the pots cost one shilling and
twopence each. In the Clarendon accounts of 1385, is a
payment of eight shillings and threepence for six gallons
of lamp oil expended on smearing various stones called
lorymers (dripstones) to keep the storms of winter from the
chimneys. In 1360 in *Gawayn and the Green Knight* 'chalk
whyt chymnees' appear on the roof of a castle; these
may have been the summits of white-washed flues. We might
note in passing that William Blake, in a picture of the
Canterbury Pilgrims, puts a large chimney smoking on a
farmhouse.

Among British chimneys to survive from the fourteenth
century are one at the Bishop's palace in Southwell, crenellated at the neck, with arcades and spire now lost; another
at Northborough Manor House, Northants, dating from

1340—it is hexagonal,. with an embattled top and ball-
flower cornice, below which each face has a gable with
crockets and finials; and a chimney at Maxstoke, whose
moulded and crenellated cap has an embattled extension—
it dates from 1348.

Chimneys begin in this century to be made plainer. With
the increase of fireplaces, twin chimneys appear. A twin
chimney at Stokesay in fact dates from the late thirteenth
century. At Clipstone in 1251, the Sheriff of Nottingham was
ordered to make a chimney in the King's wardrobe, through
a mantell and through another mantell in the queen's wardrobe "by one and the same flue". At Harlech are the remains
of a quadruple chimney-stack of the fourteenth century.
Scottish pele towers seem to have been built with chimneys, as
Kirkhope in the vale of Ettrick, Affleck in Angus, and Claypotts at Dundee.

Some lantern-type chimneys, however, continued to be
made, mainly for kitchens. Like stone louvres they were
set over great kitchens such as the Abbot's kitchen at
Glastonbury. One at West Coker served the kitchen. One
at Twywell started square, squinched itself into a hexagon,
then became octagonal as far as a round course : over this
are eight gabled triangular openings, and then another
tier of eight smaller openings; the whole terminating in a
finial.

Simone Martini in *The Road to Calvary*, painted c. 1340,
shows a louvre. The word 'louvre' can only be dated 1440
at the earliest, but many louvres survive from the previous
century. A louvre (from the French l'ouvert) is a lantern-
like structure placed on the roof over a central hearth. They
had openings at the sides, usually with louvre-boards which
could be pulled by strings, as at Marlborough in 1238,
Gloucester (1280), Hadleigh Castle (1363), and Clipstone

(1370). Some fourteenth-century louvres could actually revolve! One rested on a mortice of bronze at Moor End in 1365, and such a mortice at Westminster cost two shillings and fourpence. Louvres could be triangular, ovoid or circular. They were built with many holes, to create a draught from any direction. Canopies were made to the holes to prevent rain from getting into the building. The louvres were flanged at the sides.

Barrels "pro louvres" were purchased at Hedon in 1443 and 1481, and at Cambridge in 1415 a cask was obtained for the louver or fumerale. In 1243 at Woodstock the keeper of the manor was ordered to make three louvres; at Windsor in 1251 Godfrey de Lister was told to have a fumatorium made in the hall to carry off the smoke. In 1253 a fumerillum was to be made in the house of the King's chaplains. It will be seen that names for this device were widely interchangeable: besides louvre and louver, we have fumerarium (1292), femerallorum, fumerale, femural (1363) and femerelle (1476), as well as fumatorium and fumerillum, and fomerel. Withal in his dictionary mentions the "lovir or fomerill where the smoake passeth out". Among the disbursements of Thomas Lucas, solicitor general to Henry VII, for the erection of Little Saxham Hall in 1507, occurs a payment "to the plommer for casting and working my fummerel of lede" and there is a payment to the glazier "for 50 fete glas in my fummerelle" . . . In the Book of Wolsey's Expenses at Christ Church, Oxford, is an entry relating to the "femerell of the new kitchen". (*Promptorium Parvulorum*, p. 169).

Every trouble was taken to make the louvre attractive. A reconstruction of a square louvre can be seen at the old Deanery, Salisbury; louvres were octagonal as at Penshurst (cf. an example still extant at Lincoln College, Oxford, dating from 1437), or hexagonal as at Westminster Hall. There was a magnificent louvre at Hampton Court, and a similarly fine one is to be seen in Grimm's drawing (1781) of Cowdray. Many fine louvres were later retained as lanterns, after they were no longer needed for the escape of smoke.

A remarkable pottery louvre was discovered in Goosegate, Nottingham, in 1961. Thirty-two such roof ventilators are now known, dating from the latter part of the 13th century or the early 14th century. The Nottingham louvre is believed to date from about 1300. It is constructed of one piece with the ridge-tile, attached centrally to it, and is conical in shape. The sides of the louvre are pierced all round by three tiers of apertures, each aperture having a projecting canopy. It resembles a miniature pagoda.

There were not only pottery louvres in the 13th and 14th century. There were chimney-pots. The late Mr. G. C. Dunning collected evidence for the discovery of thirty-four such chimney-pots of baked clay from south-eastern and southern England where they were in use in the thirteenth century. They are conical, widest at the base and tapering to the top. They are mainly straight sided, though some are cylindrical and some are bellied. They were from 10 to 15 inches high, their tops are usually 4 to 5 inches across, the base is usually between 8 and 10 inches. Most had two holes in the side, opposite one another. Their tops are incised, and their sides decorated: some show extensive staining or blackening caused in use. There are two chimney-pots from London, of this period, which are of different design, short, dome shaped, very narrow at the top, and having triangular holes in the sides. Mr. Dunning says that "the special features in the design of clay chimney-pots demonstrate that the dynamics of the subject was appreciated in the early thirteenth century . . . The principles underlying the design of these chimney-pots may be stated as follows:

1. to increase the velocity of ascent of the smoke by reducing the cross-sectional area of the outlet.
2. to minimize the effect of down-draught by reducing the area acted on by the wind.
3. to promote up-draught by creating a cross-draught inside the upper part of the chimney.

"The first and second requirements were met by making the chimney-pot conical or tapering from the base upwards, and by having a comparatively small outlet hole in the top. The third requirement was met by providing small holes in the side. The complex problem of designing an efficient chimney-pot thus appears to have been solved with some success in the thirteenth century. The problem has, however, taxed the ingenuity of devisors of chimney-pots ever since, and produced a multitude of solutions more or less satisfactory in the form of tallboys, cowls, and vents, until the present day."

Of the thirty-six known mediaeval chimney-pots, twenty-four are from Sussex: from Chichester, Bosham, Lewes, Glynde, Ringmer, and Pevensey. One is from Sandwich in Kent, one from Leatherhead in Surrey; one each from Binsted and Winchester in Hants; one each from Laverstock in Wiltshire and Enborne in Berkshire, Oriel College, Oxford, and another from Deddington; and the rest from London.

Thirteenth-century cob-cottages are known to have had a clay chimney on one end, and fourteenth-century cruck-cottages a louvre over a central hearth. Wicker and thatch chimneys have survived to the present day in Carmarthen-shire and on the English-Welsh border. In appearance these buildings resembled the "smoky-houses" for fish curing on the north-east coast of Scotland, while so far as the escape of smoke is concerned they resemble the "black-houses" of which some survive in the Western Isles of Scotland, though these latter often have a chimney-pot stuck into the thatch to aid the outlet of smoke. A mediaeval hood and flue of timber and clay was in a stone house demolished at Darwen in Lancashire in 1927: chimneys are known to have been timber framed with wattle and clay; there were stout oak posts with short cross bars at intervals, the spaces between being filled with stakes and branches inter-twined like wattle work and coated with raddle and daub (as at Marley Farm, Smarden, Kent). Such chimneys were dangerous always, and fortunately rare, disappearing alto-gether or becoming obsolete with the plentiful supply of bricks in the fifteenth century. Where building materials were lacking before this date, expedients were followed, as the insertion of a barrel with both ends removed into a thatched roof, and the construction of a rectangular wooden chimney, made of notched branches and lined with a coat of clay plaster. Such chimneys as the last were made by American frontiersmen, and there is an example—rebuilt—at Fort Harrod, Harrodsburg, Kentucky. Timber chimneys of the fourteenth century have been found in England in Cambridgeshire and Huntingdonshire, in Westmorland and Lancashire. Some timber houses had smoke vents in their gables, and it has been conjectured that this might have been the origin of the common gabled hip-roof. So far as stone buildings are concerned, the hall at Minster Lovell had openings in the tops of the gable walls instead of louvres. Bolton Castle in Wensleydale has smoke outlets in the soffits of the side windows of the hall—it is thought that before these were made, the traceried heads of windows with two or more lights would be left unglazed to permit the escape of smoke.

Chimneys and pots appear in a *Nativity Scene* by Antoniazzo Romano. This is in the National Museum of Art at New York, and was painted in 1482. *October* (1413-1416) by the Limbourg brothers, shows plenty of chimneys on a chateau, all of them pillar chimneys, some single, some double. *The Portinari Altarpiece* (1476) by Hugo Van der Goes shows a chimney on a gable. In *The Duke de Berry on a Journey* (1410-1413), an illumination from the Belles Heures de Jean de France, Duc de Berry, in the National Museum of Art in New York, a castle has two rectangular and two round chimneys, the latter having neckings and cornices. Another illumination of the same date (and in the same museum), the *Story of Bruno and the Grand Chartreuse,* shows a huge church and a cloister, over which rise some twenty ark-like cells, each with a chimney of the Black Forest or gable top type. Few churches in England have mediaeval chimneys surviving, though one survives (15th-century) at Hanwell in Oxfordshire. Vestries are usually Victorian additions, and their chimneys mock-gothic. The fifteenth century was the first great century of chimney building. Dr. Margaret Wood cites fourteen major examples of surviving fifteenth-century chimneys in England. In 1425 "2,000 breke for making chemeneys at Langley" were bought at Rickmansworth. There were many chimneys in London by 1415, according to an illustration of the Tower of London from the *Poem* of Charles, Duke of Orleans, imprisoned in the Tower after Agincourt. Place Farm, Tisbury, Wilts, has a late fifteenth-century chimney terminating in a spire : but spires were usually by this time

truncated or replaced by low caps. The familiar fifteenth-
century chimney is an octagonal shaft, usually long and
slender, with an open crenellated top at first, later merely
moulded. The crenellation was often out-turned (plate 4).
Many fifteenth-century chimneys in France have crowns of
iron spikes, and a notable survival is that at the Chateau de
Sully, on the Loire. A square type of chimney also appears
in the fifteenth century. There is a square crenellated chimney at Great Chalfield in Wiltshire. At Castle Cottage,
Great Bedwyn in the same county (plate 5) a square
stone stack survives with a cylindrical chimney-shaft of
Norman type, but of the fifteenth century or the very end
of the fourteenth : it and the surrounding wall are all that
remains of the original house. The most magnificent brick
chimneys of this century are to be seen at Tattershall,
Thornbury Castle, Layer Marney in Essex and East Barsham
manor in Norfolk.

Chimneys were still not common till the reign of Elizabeth
I, but by the end of the sixteenth century most houses, including the houses of the peasants, had acquired chimney stacks.
A chimney stack, ending in an attractive-looking cap,
became a popular feature everywhere, added outside existing walls—where the projecting hearth disappeared, to be
replaced by a deeply recessed fireplace—or incorporated
into a gable-end. A room without a chimney was considered
unfit for guests! But there is another line on this matter.
Harrison in Holinshed's *Chronicle* (1577-87) speaks of
"increase of chimneys because all want them"; hitherto
only the houses of the rich and religious houses, sported
chimneys. He adds "Now have we many chimneys, and
yet our tenderlings complain of rheumes, catarrhs, and
poses. Then had we none but reredoses, and our heads
did never ake. For as the smoke in those daies was supposed

to be a sufficient hardening for the timber of the house, so it was reputed a far better medicine to keepe the good man and his familie from the quacke or pose, wherewith as then verie few were oft acquainted".

The chief fashion in this century was for several brick stacks on one stack; usually four on a square base. The stacks were octagonal, hexagonal, square, circular, fluted, reeded, and spiral; they were decorated with chevrons, zigzags, diamonds, honeycombs, and heraldic badges. Typical Tudor chimneys may be seen at Gainsborough Old Hall, Lincolnshire; St. Osyth Priory, Essex; Kirby Hall, Northants; Cobham Hall, Kent; and in the village of Newport, Essex. Many such chimneys date from the reign of Henry VIII, a very showy age. The even more famous chimneys of, e.g., Compton Wynyates and Oxburgh Hall, owe their existence to the local material which was handy, Midland Clay. The bricks for these chimneys had to be moulded and shaped by hand before going into the kiln. The making of brick chimneys was a real craft. It seems the brick maker could outdo the stonemason, and there are many stone houses of this period with ornamental brick chimneys. This art came from the Low Countries.

At Collyweston in 1504 a deficiency in the redness of the bricks was helped out with "stuff brought for the colering of the cheney of Brike; vij lb. of red ocker with 1 oz. of the offales of the glovers lether, xijd. Item to John Bradley wiff for xiiij gallons of small ale for the said cheney of bryk, vjd." In 1511 the building of Church House at Great Sherston, Wilts, included a chimney of free stone with a top of free stone. Was this latter a pot? In about 1525 at Hengrave Hall, Suffolk, one Jhon Eastawe had "to make of roubed brick all the schank of the chymines". In 1532 at Westminster "tonnellis" were "hewn for chimnies together with heads and bases" : these were stone chimneys. Nonsuch Palace (begun 1538) is pictured with a large number of funnel-shaped chimneys. To this century belong the chimneys of Montacute (1588), and—far more important—the great forest of chimneys on the Chateau de Chambord (plate 6) whose nearest rivals in France are the Chateau de Maisons near Paris and the Chateau de Blois.

The positioning of chimneys in Tudor times was an important part of the symmetrical design of the building. It is the half timbered houses of the Kent Weald which show best the evolution of the positioning of chimneys. These houses were built on a flat H-plan. The common living room was in the centre, open to the roof. About 1550, floors began to be inserted seven to nine feet above the ground floor, the hall being thereby converted into a ground and a first floor. At the same time, a chimney stack was built, as a great opening on the ground floor (from 4 feet by 8 to 6 feet by 14), with one or more windows in the outer wall, and with a cambered oak beam to act as a lintel in the side of the room, thereby making an inglenook. In this people sat, and bacon and hams were smoked in the huge cavity above, which ran straight upwards, narrowing as it neared the top. Sir Reginald Blomfield says of this arrangement that it was "admirably picturesque, but better adapted for down-draughts and for smoking bacon than for the purposes of a chimney". The upper part of this stack was square; or if several flues were gathered together, the top was of octagonal shafts (as at East Barsham (plates 7 & 8) and Hampton Court), the higher, the more to counteract down draughts. We are not to pass by, in this survey, the many magnificent stepped and buttressed chimneys of the 16th-century stone houses of Yorkshire and Lancashire. In one of these, at Shibden Hall, Halifax, a chamber for smoking bacon was built round the hall chimney-stack.

A circular and battlemented chimney is portrayed in Hans Bol's *Town Panorama* (1578). Giorgione's *The Tempest* (1505) shows funnel-shaped chimneys. Breughel the Elder's *The Return of the Hunters* (1565) shows two or three chimneys having—conjecturally—chimney-pots on them. His *The Blind Leading the Blind* (1568) shows two chimney-stacks.

The seventeenth-century English house was built round a massive internal stack. This gave support to the building and made possible the use of shorter timbers. It lent dignity to the house, as we can see today from many houses of this period in Surrey, Kent, Sussex, and Essex (plates 9, 38, 39). It was the principal feature of the house and often the most expensive. It is "still one of the most notable features of our domestic architecture and represents perhaps the most charming of all vernacular contributions to the era of the Renaissance" (Braun). The stack carried the flues of four fireplaces. The early seventeenth-century stack was ornate, as may be seen from many a Sussex and Kent farmhouse. There were also ornate stacks still being built on sixteenth-century lines, as at Great Wigsell and at Bodiam (here there were five shafts, including a larger one in the middle). Notable are the great tea-caddy chimneys of Clare College, Cambridge; Thorpe Hall, Peterborough; Coleshill (Berks; destroyed) and Sudbury Hall, Derbyshire. Oddly enough such chimneys were not always built on sound foundations; they sometimes rested on timber. In stone-building areas side stacks continued, rising from the roof flush with the wall space, and provided with a ridged span connecting them with the main roof. We

c

should note the chimneys, disguised as pillars, at Burghley House and Kirby Hall. By the end of the 17th century there had evolved the valley-roof with two big stacks containing four flues each; a little later, side stacks and hipped roofs. By this time stacks had become plainer; they were rectangular or cruciform and had thick cornices.

It is strange that chimney stacks play no part in views of Chatsworth, Castle Howard, or Blenheim; in the last named they are disguised. Holland House is shown in 1606-7 as without any chimneys at all. Conversely Wilton House suffers from a number of chimneys inconsequential in themselves, ugly, and indiscriminately placed.

Many mediaeval houses were 'modernized' as to their chimney arrangements in this century. All felt they had to have them. Chimneys became status-symbols. Charles II taxed them, but they were considered such important status-symbols that the taxes were willingly paid. Chimneys were accordingly made to look larger, and many false stacks were built. Yet, in Scotland in 1662, many 'ordinary country houses are pitiful cots, built of stone and covered with turves, having in them one room, many of them no chimneys'.

The chimneys of the French Renaissance were built lofty, to match the high roofs. The chimneys of the German Renaissance, necessary for heat in a cold climate, had to be prominent features. In Italy chimneys continued to be masked, except at Venice. This city is famed for its quite tall and ubiquitous funnel-shaped chimneys; cold winds from the sea and the mountains made these essential.

In many rectangular chimneys of this period, the top courses projected to form protective caps. The cap was generally a brickwork version of Classical entablature. Anne Hathaway's cottage has chimneys with tall and prominent caps surmounted by a narrowing brick structure. The more massive early chimneys were often decorated with bevels or pilasters. This type was used as the central feature of the colonial New England farmhouse. The end position was customary for chimneys in the warmer southern colonies, allowing for better air circulation through the house, and less retention of heat by the chimney. Later, end-placement of fireplaces, which could easily be combined to form fire-proof party walls, became the standard for row housing everywhere.

It had by now been discovered that flues need to be close together, and need not be so big: by the middle of the seventeenth century chimney-stacks had developed into plain, compact, rectangular affairs. Flues were made smaller, the size of chimney-openings was reduced, till they reached the exiguous dimensions induced by the modern grate.

Cornelius Cort, a Dutch painter of the 17th century, depicts all kinds of chimneys; he shows one grouped stack, and possibly a pot. Van Goyer in his *Village* (1626) shows a chimney top of the Dorset or Black Forest type with an overlapping slate and a stone to keep it in place: he shows a pot on a cottage near the church. A Dorset or Black Forest type and a gabled chimney are shown in Blomaert's *The Farm* (1650). A number of seventeenth-century Dutch painters show chimneys of this kind, and pots. Look carefully at Vermeer's famous *View of Delft*. Rubens in his *Landscape with the Chateau of Steen* (1636) gives his castle at least one tall chimney stack with a greatly projecting cornice.

The eighteenth century is notable, from the point of view of this survey, for the widespread introduction in England of chimney-pots. They were unnecessary in chimneys with straight flues—of such a type that you could stand in the fireplace and look right up them to the sky— but became essential with the growing introduction of bends into flues, to procure additional draught. "In times when coal was more plentiful than it is now", wrote Mr. Edward Roper in The Times in 1956, "and fires more generously made up, volleys of smoke often spoiled the furnishings and choked the Victorian householders whose homes the pots adorned. A good deal more is now known about the design of flues, but the eddies of wind over sloping roofs have never been predictable even by experienced architects, and correc- tive treatment was applied by means of the chimney- pot." The height to which the chimney—and chimney-pot— projects affects the performance of the flue and chimney by influencing pressure variations set up by wind. The use of ready-made chimney-pots was the result of the necessity of adding to existing chimneys for the purpose of increased draught. The introduction of pots of greater length—from 3′ 6″ up to 6′ 0″—met proven necessities. The term 'Tallboy' was used by manufacturers and builders to describe these larger pots, which did so much to lengthen stacks for purposes of draught. Tallboys were—and are— frequently used to counteract the effect on draught of an adjacent higher building—or even high chimney-pot.

The *Encyclopaedia Britannica's* only mention of chimney- pots is as follows :

"Flues should be vertical except where bends are necessary. Usually the flue-lining is carried a few inches above the masonry of a chimney-stack, and a cement bevel sloped up to it. Baffles, hoods, cowls, chimney-pots, or spark arrestors, may form part of the chimney-top to control venting. A capstone will keep rain out of a seldom used flue."

The purpose of chimney-pots, says R. Barry (in his *Construction of Buildings*), is to provide a smooth outlet to the top of flues to allow the smoke to rise freely, and to raise the level of the outlet for the smoke above the stack whose height is restricted by regulation. The purpose is to prevent down-draught. Down-draught is caused by surrounding buildings or trees which are higher than the stack. Where the extent of the down-draught cannot be forecast, a variety of tallboys and revolving terminals are manufactured to eliminate or minimize the effect of down-draught. Chimney-pots have to be flaunched around (with a mixture of coarse sand, cement, and water) to keep the pots in position and throw off water.

Contemporary drawings of new streets in Bath (very early 18th century) show chimneys and occasional pots, some of these very tall. We have seen that Breughel and Vermeer had depicted chimney-pots; these were mostly small ones. Zuccari in a picture (1590) of himself at work on the scaffolding of a palace, watched by Michaelangelo, shows chimneys and some pots. A. Van Dyck in a picture of 1632 of Charles I and his wife and two eldest children, shows chimneys and quite tall pots in the background. We have already seen that pots had been used on the Continent for some centuries, but Van Dyck was mistaken in attributing them to England at this date.

In 1709 an Act of Parliament was passed forbidding timber to be nearer than five inches to any chimney flue or fireplace, and that all flues should be plastered or pargeted from bottom to top.

In the 18th century the chimney-stack came to be neglected. Architects had ceased to consider it an essential of the elevation. It was a necessary evil, to be kept in the background as much as possible. Certainly the Georgians

wanted to remove the central stack and replace it with
gable stacks: a cupola often took the place of the central
stack in the design. The gable stacks were internal, within
the walls, not to spoil the symmetry of the external elevation.

Nathaniel Lloyd considered that the widespread introduction of chimney-pots into England originated with the
circulation of *Fires Improved* by M. Gauger (1713), made
English and improved by J. T. Desagulièrs M.A., F.R.S.,
London 1715. This book illustrates 'the earliest pots', square
and tapering: good examples of them can be seen on a
house on the north west side of the Close at Wells. Lloyd
adds that with the 18th century came decadence of chimney
design, by the invention of chimney-pots of various forms.
Whereas before the era of pots, chimneys were built in the
proportions of a column or pedestal, the cap of which was
the crowning feature, the pot required only a sufficiently
sound base upon which it could be fixed "well flaunched
up and weathered in cement"; the result was that in
most buildings the chimney cap was replaced by a shallow
projecting band. By 1780, Lloyd says, chimney-pots had
"attained an ugliness scarcely surpassed by modern inven-
tions", and gives an illustration from *An Essay on Chimneys*
by Robert Clavering (London, 1779) depicting a primitive
Lobster-back sporting a dragon showing its teeth, instead
of the arrow or direction-finder usually surmounting these
cowls. *A Treatise on Preventing Fires Smoaking* was published
in 1715, and refers to 'the new chimney'. This is not the
Cheminée de Nancy to be mentioned later, and we are
left wondering to what special pot it referred.

Canaletto, the most chimney-conscious of all great artists,
shows pots in London in 1746, from which can be picked
out square flue-terminals and some very tall tallboys.

The diary of the visits of John Yeoman to London

(1774-7) mentions a visit to the house "where the tun potts are made". Pots he describes as being made there have caps, the smoke escaping through holes in the sides or through horns sprouting downwards in the sides.

John Constable depicts chimney-pots in *The Haywain* and in *A Cornfield with Figures*. There is a drawing of his of Fitzroy Square in London (1795), which shows a good London skyline of chimney-pots.

So we come to the year 1796 and the publication of the Essay by Sir Benjamin Thompson (then Count Rumford), *Of Chimney Fireplaces, and the Principles of Chimney-construction,* which was a landmark, and a now firmly recognized landmark, in the history of the chimney. Count Rumford's principles were used 'to treat successfully over 500 defective fireplaces in London'. As a result the Lord Provost and Magistrates of Edinburgh 'voted a sum of money to defray the expenses of a bricklayer, who is to be sent for the purpose of establishing the same plan in that city'. Rumford instructed this man, and conceived the idea of publishing his essay. He made no patent. Little attention was given to Rumford's thesis over the next one hundred and fifty years, until very recently, when, with rationing and the high price of coal compelling people to take more care, fireplaces began to be improved on Rumford's lines. Briefly, these were his principles:

1. A sloped fire-back.
2. A streamlined lintel to lead the room air into the flue without encumbrance.
3. A deep and narrow throat, placed centrally above the grate, four inches wide and six to eight inches deep: the entrance to the throat to be rounded.

4. A flat smoke-shelf, level with the top of the throat, to stop soot and rain.

5. A small smoke-chamber.

6. Splayed sides and a decided narrowing of the fireplace towards the back. The flue should run from the smoke-chamber to the chimney-pot as straightly as possible, any unavoidable bends being slow and smoothly turned. The sharp kink often introduced is a cause of down-draught.

We would like to know more of the Cheminée de Nancy, in use since 1738, of which the following is written by W. Bernan, in *The History and Art of Warming and Ventilating* (London, 1845): "The moderate cost and simple con-struction of the Cheminée de Nancy adapt it above all others to the use of the cottager or to situations where it is inconvenient to make alterations on the hearth of the recess. What a world of comfort would not this simple apparatus produce in an English cottage, as a substitute for the ache-breeding, fuel-wasting grates, with gaping flues and buried in brickwork, that throw away three-quarters of the heat of all the fuel consumed in them".

From this golden age of chimney-pots where does a sufficient number survive, to attract our notice? The only infallible advice that can be given is to search Georgian buildings and Georgian towns. Be on the look out when old property is being demolished—if you can, beat the house-breakers and save the pots, which is extremely difficult. The old pots are hand-made and bear the marks of the potters' wheel and in some cases a maker's mark. They will be weathered, possibly a little mis-shapen, they may be faded and discoloured—though many are made of a rich terra cotta which it seems cannot lose its lustre. Happy

hunting grounds for old pots are London (23, 25, 29),
Reading, Brighton (12 & 27), Chichester (plates 13-22 & 37),
Fareham, Hungerford, Bath and York. Straight tallboys,
of a shorter or longer length, characterize London, tapering
tallboys Brighton and Bath; while the Chichester-Fareham
area specialises in handsome pots—one variety of red
terra cotta, pierced with holes near the apex (plate 16);
another variety of lighter hue, adorned with a band of
white 'slip' below the top (plates 14, 16 & 22); and yet
another variety, much shorter and much rarer, is of a
slug pellet shape, looks as if it had been painted white
over red, and bears very distinctly the marks of the potters'
wheel (plate 25). It is worthwhile also looking carefully at all
older horned or sprouted pots, especially examples in the
Chichester[1] area and in South Wales.

Old pots cannot, on the whole, be identified from contemporary drawings or etchings; the artists would not go into
sufficient detail, they would merely 'indicate' pots or draw
pots according to a vague general concept. Early pictures
do however show pots and cowls at Bath, and large square
pots. Early pictures of Richmond, Surrey, show these last,
and also a number of chimney coverings of the Lakeland
two-slate variety. *Ancient Reliques* (London 1813), shows
fairly large chimney-pots in London, and one simple example
of a lobster-back cowl; it shows a very long chimney-stack
at St. Bartholomew's Hospital, surmounted all along by
Lakeland two-slate devices. The same book shows, at

---

[1] A walk round the city walls of Chichester will reveal as great a
selection of pots as can be seen anywhere at that convenient viewing
height. A visit to the potteries at Wrecclesham and (until its recent
demolition) at Fareham reveals a part source of these pots, and explains
the nickname of 'Long Farehams' given to many of them. These potteries
date back to the year 1700 A.D. There are one or two examples of their
pots still in existence. Harting Manor proudly exhibited one of these
until fairly recently.

Framlingham Castle, old chimneys and a modern stack
with pots: it shows pots, much the same as in London, at
Bristol, Shrewsbury, and Cambridge; shorter pots in Trow-
bridge and Aylesford; and at Liverpool a smaller circular
plastered stack on top of a square stack—we shall see that this
is in fact a speciality of West Sussex.

What of the chimney and the chimney-pot in, say,
Nash's architecture? Contemporary pictures show very tall
chimney-pots on the great chimney-stacks of Park Crescent,
Sussex Place, Regents Park and other places in London.
At Royal Lodge, Windsor, there are tall hexagonal pillar
chimneys and diamond-wise decorated pillar chimneys,
with pots on each, and multiple pillar chimney-stacks (See
also plate 12).

J. W. Hiort, in 1826, issued a 47 page *Practical Treatise
on the Construction of Chimneys,* "containing an examination
of the common mode in which they are built, with an
accurate description of the newly invented tunnel, demon-
strating its utility and safety, its importance in superseding
the painful practice of employing climbing-boys, the remedy
which it affords for the nuisance of smokey flues, and the
advantages to be derived from its rendering those lofty
shafts, with their numerous unsightly contrivances at present
in use, entirely unnecessary; together with complete in-
structions for its adoption, whereby a competent judgement
may be formed of the causes which prevent the free
ascent of smoke in chimneys, and workmen may be enabled
to apply a cure for so serious an evil". The large flues
of 14 inches by 9 inches—for boys to climb—are no
good, Hiort says; 9 inches square is sufficient. Pargetting
of flues is useless, fire-plaster is perishable. Turn caps and
wind-guards are useless, for not only is the mouth of
the chimney affected by winds, but so is the whole stack,

especially when mortar and bricks are in a decayed state, the flue at the end of the stack being specially vulnerable. Turns in flues are bad, high stacks are dangerous and cause down-draughts, and pots should not be circular.

What was Hiort's remedy? Circular flues were to be used, old chimneys were to be topped with a projecting cornice, sloped and weathered. The wind striking on this took an upward direction, and assisted the emission of smoke. Instead of 'pots, cowls, and whimsical contrivances' Hiort advocated a cylinder of cast iron on top of the stack, enclosed in a shaft of hexagonal form consisting of gauged club-bricks or stone.

In the same year, 1826, was invented a scandiscope or mechanical device for sweeping chimneys. The Every Day Book of May 1, 1826, shows a cartoon depicting garlanded boy chimney-sweeps dancing round this device in joy at their release from a sad and painful employment. The cartoon is headed *The Last Chimney Sweeper*, a description of the device follows, and below comes the rhyme:

> Some wooden tubes, a brush, and rope
>   Are all you need employ;
> Pray order, maids, the Scandiscope,
>   And not the climbing boy.

The Scandiscope was "a large brush made of a number of small whalebone sticks, fastened into a round ball of wood, and extending in most cases to a diameter of two feet" which "is thrust up the chimney by means of hollow cylinders or tubes, fitting into one another like the joints of a fishing-rod, with a long cord running through them; it is worked up and down, as each fresh joint is added, until it reaches the chimney-pot; it is then shortened joint by

joint, and on each joint being removed, it is in like
manner worked up and down in its descent; and thus
you have your chimney swept perfectly clean by this
machine."

A society for the abolition of chimney-sweeping by small
boys, had as its Patron King George IV, and strongly
commended the Scandiscope. But for a long time it failed
in its object. A boastful and complacent 'Society of Master
Chimney Sweepers' advertised their kindness and humanity
to their poor apprentices by giving them a splendid dinner,
at the Eyre Arms in St. John's Wood, on May 1, 1826
publicly advertised and preceded by a triumphal procession
of clean and healthy looking young sweeps; at the after-
dinner speeches the Scandiscope came in for some scathing
criticism.

It was not only the campaign against chimney-sweeping
by human instruments that failed in its object. Mr. Hiort's
debunking of the chimney-pot (see above) failed so badly
that the Victorian era was notable for an unprecedented pro-
liferation of chimney-pots, and of types, sizes, and shapes
of chimney-pots. Everything is an antique which is a hundred years old, and we shall be looking in detail at
the principal varieties of these chimney pots in another
chapter. Some are by now obsolete, but most are still visible
on the tops of houses, and a considerable number are still
being manufactured, especially in the Midlands and North
of England.

Meanwhile, what is the present attitude to chimney-pots,
and what are the present theories?

A. Clifton Taylor, in *The Pattern of English Building*,
written in 1962, dislikes chimney-pots. He cannot see any
reason for them, and quotes the old question of Tennyson
(see p. 14). Like many other technical experts, he regards

round or square flue terminals (lengths of drainpipes pro-
truding above the stack to a height of little more than two
inches) as ideal. He considers the pot or its substitute should
be invisible from below.

"Pots" says Mackay, in *Building Construction,* "are not
always necessary", and their omission is sometimes preferred.
The best type, in his opinion, would be cylindrical, 8 or 9
inches in diameter inside, half to three quarters of an inch
thick, and flanged at the base. They should be a foot high,
tapered to an internal measurement of $7\frac{1}{2}$ inches at the
top, to increase the velocity of the ascending current.
The pot should be securely built in cement mortar between
two or three courses of brickwork (or a stone cap or several
courses of tiles): the top of the stack should be flaunched,
to throw off water. "Many buildings", he says, "are marred
by unsightly chimneys which penetrate the roofs at random.
As a rule, stacks should be of simple design. A frequent
mistake is to complete stacks with cappings of oversailing
courses with excessive projection. He speaks of "the coarse
finish which these give . . . Ugly chimney pots are common.
Tall chimney-pots are unnecessary, unless the flues are
short or have been improperly constructed, or high trees
or buildings are in such close proximity as to produce
down-draughts. An unobtrusive but effective finish may
be obtained if the chimney-pots (or short lengths of drainpipes!) are caused to project not more than an inch
above the flaunching: this is usually sufficient to prevent
eddies of wind which may be created if the top surfaces
of the stacks are flat".

Percy L. Marks, in *Chimneys and Flues* (London 1935),
speaks of the importance of helping the up-draught, and
preventing damp from entering the chimney. Lean and
lanky chimneys are unsightly, and an extra thickness of

walling is desirable. "Chimney-stacks" he says "are apt to
assert their presence with undue emphasis, and the skyline
may be quite spoilt as a result". The gathering together
of flues is desirable, for it improves up-draught. In the small
house, indeed, 'this has a very happy result at times'.
Every endeavour should be made to impart as much artistic
appearance as possible to chimney-stacks. He commends
Vanbrugh, who disguised chimney-stacks as urns and
vases. Anaemic alignment must be avoided, and an attempt
made to produce variety. All this, which presumably would
not spoil the skyline, is excellent. Marks then quotes
Lloyd's principles of stack-design, as follows :-

The slighter the shaft, the less should be the projections.
The thicker the bricks, the less should they project.
A shaft square in cross-section will take oversailing
courses of wider projection than a merely rectangular shaft
of unequal sides.
A shaft on a gable end looks best at right angles to
the ridge.
A shaft issuing through the roof looks best when its longer
axis is parallel to the ridge.
The beauty of the shaft is greatly increased by judicious
vertical breaks.
Shafts wide on elevation and very thin on return will
not carry heavy caps.
The addition of pots is destructive of design.

Marks adds that tallboys are unsightly, and create an
obstruction to free the up-draught of adjacent flues, except
when they surmount an isolated chimney.
He considers as good treatment for chimney capping,
a solid top, the flue venting horizontally beneath (this is the

vernacular use of Wiltshire and Dorset and the Black Forest);
while in so far as he condescends to admit pots, he allows
louvred pots with solid tops.

So the chimney-pot is disliked, debunked, and dethroned :
but it persists in dominating our skyline. It is only because
its disappearance is ultimately possible, if not certain, that
we are so concerned to draw the attention of the student
and general reader to it; for perhaps no craft has declined
so unsung and so unrecorded.

Chapter Three

STACKS, POTS, AND COWLS.

A.

During a visit to the United States some years ago, my kind hostess was driving me through Richmond, Virginia. "Don't you miss the chimney-pots?" she suddenly asked. I replied that no one could miss them more. For Britain leads the world in chimneys and chimney-pots, in quantity, size, conspicuousness, and sheer artistry. "Edward Whymper, travelling in the Andes in 1879, and pondering over the strange and dull appearance of the city of Quito, finally attributed it to the absence of chimneys" (Laurence Wright, *Home Fires Burning*).

It may not have been Britain's idea at first. We have seen that chimneys and chimney-pots were probably used in some European countries before they were in Britain, and it may be that chimney-pots were twice in history introduced into Britain from abroad—in the thirteenth and in the eighteenth centuries.

Whether you would miss the chimney-pots or not, whether you consider that Britain leads the world or not, depends on your powers of observation. Once again, go up high in a big city, and study the intensely varied and characterful skyline, and notice the large part played in this by chimney-stacks and pots. London with its many tallboys and donkey-leg cowls at frequent intervals: Paris with its long stacks athwart the roof ridges and its much smaller but characteristic chimney-pots, punctuated as often as in London by tin cowls, so often ending in 'Chinese-hats'. Go up a hill overlooking a congested area of one of our industrial towns, and see the long rows, the monotonous rows, not just of houses, but of utterly similar chimney-stacks and pots, street after street built with one design of stack surmounted in all cases by the same number and the same style of pots. Look at the smarter surburban scene, and see something similar—trees alone breaking up the monotonous rooftop and chimneyscape scene. One street, or estate, will have nothing but thousands of insignificant flue-terminals; another may have on every house a thickset central stack with six red bellied pots. Look at the typical village scene. On your left is the great house with its four massive Georgian tea-caddy stacks; beyond it is the school with its Victorian mock-Tudor chimneys; opposite is the Vicarage with conspicuous Victorian gothic chimneys having foliated ornament and flue terminals instead of pots; between it and the old inn is a twentieth-century bungalow having a stack at each end surmounted by tallboys—or by one tallboy and a shorter red pot. The eighteenth-century inn has magnificent and shapely and slender chimneys crowned irregularly by one or more handsome terra cotta pots. Look at two country scenes. One is dominated by a little bottle-shaped toll house with its one small pillar chimney rising out of its round roof: behind it at the end of a drive is the old farm with its massive central chimney-stack rising centrally from a roof of Horsham stone. Further north is the little but and ben, a modest and plain stack rising out of the gables of both but and ben, surmounted in the one case by a plain white pot covered with a decent hat, and in the other by a flue terminal capped by a revolving 'Granny'. The great house opposite is surmounted

D

by a long chimney stack that faces the road bearing twelve tapering white pots, while smaller chimney-stacks, many with more than one 'Granny' are to be seen on the roofs of the wings.

What a difference the absence of chimneys and chimney-pots would make to these scenes!

Moreover, time would fail one if I were to tell of Boiler chimneys, Bakehouse chimneys, Brewery chimneys, Cornish tin-mine chimneys, and the Yorkshire lead-mine chimneys which rise forlornly and abandonedly out of the moors. There is no space in this book for Mill chimneys, for the forest of tall stacks, round and square, that make the chief skyline of Yorkshire and Lancashire industrial towns, or for the great ornamented chimneys like Cox's Italianate chimney at Dundee. Nevertheless these too want watching, for they are fast thinning out (see plate 29). I cannot speak of Crematorium chimneys, which are blossoming out on new and original lines intended to mask their true purpose. I cannot give space to Power Station chimneys, once the greatest of all but now dwarfed by Television towers. But I would draw the reader's attention to the great armies of Brickfield chimneys which surround Bletchley and Peterborough.

B.

Chimney-stacks in Great Britain are normally either axial, at gable-ends, or lateral; there is also a common use in vernacular architecture in the south-west, especially in Devon, in which the chimney backs on the cross passage, or stands in the front of the house (plate 28, S. Devon). There are, as with chimney-pots, considerable regional differences so far as the type and positioning of stacks is concerned. Mr. R. W. Barley, in *The English Farmhouse and*

Cottage (London, 1961), brings this out strongly. In the south-east, there are massive brick axial stacks, rising square above the ridge of the roof. South of the Thames, these chimney-stacks are finished with oversailing courses. In East Anglia they are finished more often with diagonal chimney-stacks or zigzag chimney-stacks, with more angles than flues. In East Anglia since Tudor times no vernacular house has been built without an axial stack. Staffordshire was fifty years behind East Anglia in starting this practice. In Herefordshire the chimney-stacks were external, but became axial by the time of James I. In the stone areas, the axial stack between two rooms never became popular, but the axial stack was to some extent taken over after 1600. The front stacks may be seen in Devon, Cornwall, and between Exmoor and the North coast of Somerset : they are plentiful at Otterton, S. Devon (plate 28). The earliest of these are late Elizabethan, and the fashion of building them lasted a century. Pride must have suggested the building of these front chimneys, often in different and more expensive material, where every passer-by could see them. They could serve only the hall and a chimney above. In all cases they were adjacent to the passage, and there was a small window in the chimney-corner, through which callers could be observed. It is worth observing that in Devon there was often a smoking chamber, for bacon, alongside the fireplace, with an opening from the fireplace at the low level, and a flue passing from its corbelled roof to the main chimney. The cream oven was further away, because of the risk of dirt.

Plain chimney-stacks without pots are the vogue in East Anglia and quite common in other parts of Britain; also in Scandinavia and particularly in the U.S.A., where stacks can be most magnificent (vide infra) and pots are

an utter rarity. A chimney stack topped by four brick
'legs' at the four corners supporting a slate or square of
stone is common in the south of England from the weald
of Sussex into Wiltshire (plate 35): it is, on a smaller
scale, the standard form of chimney in the Black Forest and
common over much of central Europe. Gable-top chimney-
stacks are common in Northern Europe, and in England
they have their prototype in the magnificent chimney-stack
at Abingdon Abbey (plate 1).

Among fine chimney-stacks should be noted in the first
place the many splendid brick chimneys of England. We
observe the dignity of all 16th- and 17th-century central
stacks. Brick of course resisted fire better than almost any
stone. As to ornamental chimneys, in the reign of Henry
VIII chimney-builders were competitive, they were real
craftsmen who were often sent for from a long distance.
Most of these ornamental brick shafts have a necking, most
of them have a cap which links together the shafts on one
stack; this cap is corbelled out in thin bricks. Of all
ornamental chimneys, the scalloped octagon is the most
interesting. These ornamental chimneys were a purely
English development; they were done in red brick, and
they are mostly in East Anglia, though there are exceptions
to this—notably Hampton Court (1515) and Thornbury
Castle, Gloucestershire (1514). The craft did not last.
Nor did many of the stacks. Many have needed restoration
and rebuilding. But imitation of this craft was widespread in the nineteenth century. Almost the whole village
of Albury, Surrey, built on an estate design in the late 1870s',
is adorned with fanciful and faithful copies of Tudor brickwork chimneys at their most elaborate.

We may note next the seventeenth-century fashion
for setting shafts anglewise on stacks, as at Bateman's,

Burwash. Rampyndene in the same village should however next be observed for its splendid square panelled
chimney-stacks (cf. Church House at Goudhurst); and we
should notice the many beautiful arcaded chimney-stacks
on Caroline and Georgian houses. Examples of these are to
be seen at Walrus Farm, Surrey, Barton Mills and Scole
in Suffolk, and on the old Woodyates Inn—being demolished
at the time of writing—ten miles south of Salisbury on the
road to Blandford (plate 11).

Gothick chimneys are plentiful. Strawberry Hill Gothick
had its own version of fifteenth- and sixteenth-century
chimneys, and they are a pleasant addition to the landscape
wherever they are found.

England's finest chimney-stacks include the round chim-
neys of the Lake District (plate 28); the buttressed lateral
stacks on old farmhouses in the West Riding and in East
Lancashire; the simple and dignified stone stacks of the
Cotswolds (plate 32); the tall brick stacks on the Midland
Clay and in Norfolk; the Georgian tea-caddies (some panelled and some arcaded) from Wiltshire to Clare College,
Cambridge; the beautifully variant central stacks on old
Wealden houses in Sussex, Surrey and Kent; the plainer
stacks of Buckinghamshire (plate 34) and Berkshire; and
the many different kinds of stack that grace East Anglia
(plates 38 & 39). There is nothing like any of these abroad,
unless in the U.S.A., in Virginia and New England especially; we shall treat of these last-named later.

Finally, we should note two curiosities. Round about
Chichester you see occasionally a crooked chimney-stack,
the bend in the flue being external, near the top (plate 36):
this seems to be a speciality of the Chichester district, and is
Georgian in origin, but I have seen a Victorian specimen in
Brighton, and a simple Georgian example at West

Shefford, Berks. At Iver, Bucks, there is a kitchen chimney which, the kitchen having no rooms above it, is joined to the main part of the house by a curved buttress up which the smoke ascends. It is at Kingsley House, Thorney Lane North, Iver. The other curiosity is the splendid round chimney we meet so often in North Devon and Somerset; it begins square from the ground, and changes to round at roof level (plate 28, Exmoor). It figures in many well known West Country views, especially of Porlock and Selworthy.

C.

In the catalogue of the National Clayware Federation, dated 1964, there are nearly five hundred varieties of chimney-pot. Of these the majority are varieties which have been in use a century or more. There is still a number of factories making chimney-pots, principally in the Midland Clay belt and in the North of England. In the south of England, extensive chimney-pot manufacture was carried on at Reading, London, Fareham, Parkstone, and Bridgwater; there is little manufacture of chimney-pots in the south of England today, but how well the former products have lasted should be evident enough to anyone visiting London, Brighton, Reading, Chichester, Bath and some parts of Norfolk.

The catalogue of the National Clayware Federation, on which we have based the following list of standard chimney-pots, shows 102 varieties (and far more sizes) of plain round chimney-pots; 147 of ornamental round chimney-pots; 67 of louvres, Bishops and windguards; 60 of square pots; and 54 of octagonal pots. Red Bank Products, Measham, near Burton on Trent, show 119 varieties in all; Doulton's of Wilnecote, near Tamworth, show 66 in all, so do Wragg's

of Swadlincote; Kinson Pottery at Parkstone show 36
varieties, and Cumberworth in Yorkshire 15, this last-
named making salt-glazed pots. These provide a good
cross section of chimney-pot manufacturers and of their
products, of which the principal are as follows :-

The tapered roll-top; the plain-roll taper; the roll-top
with square base or flanged base or roll base. The ornamental roll-top.

The plain roll, two roll, three roll, dwarf roll, the moulded
roll, the three grooved roll, the London roll, the broad-
shouldered roll, the four ring hooded roll.

The plain tapered : special roll tapered, roll tapered.

The plain flue lining, beaded flue lining, oval flue lining,
square tapered flue lining (called at Cumberworth 'the
Quaker pot'), square flue lining.

The plain beehive, pocket beehive, key-pattern beehive,
4-ring beehive, ornamental beehive, fluted beehive, horned
beehive.

The cannon-head, beaded cannon-head, flanged cannon-
head, special cannon-head.

The plain taper; or beaded, moulded, hooded taper.

The bellied pot (several varieties).

The Dublin can.

The Bishop : square Bishop, two piece (= Windguard
square base of Doulton's, and looks more like the King on a
chessboard than a bishop).

The Bell-top.

The tulip. Its spikes bend outward.

The square panelled; square spiked; plain square; square
taper; square with 3, 4, 5 or 6 rings; square hooded;
crowned square; and in all 60 varieties of square pots. An
old square pot, with vertical openings on the four sides,
can be seen on a farmhouse in Rushmore Park, Wilts, on

a cottage 2 miles away, and over a gate into Salisbury
Cathedral Close: but as far as I know, nowhere else.
   The fluted round pot: the ornamental fluted.
   The round spiked pot.
   The round pot (24 varieties); the round top (3 varieties).
54 kinds of octagon, several spiked, several castellated,
several ornamental (some like small-scale models of Tudor
chimney-shafts).
   The down-draught cure = 'the Champion' = the smokecure = the Regis = the "A" (Ensor's catalogue). Resembles
a jelly-mould.
   The popular down-draught cure, fireclay, tin, straight,
and bellied = Kay's Patent chimney-pot. A schoolboy name
for this chimney-pot is a donkey-leg. It provides most of the
skyline in several London suburbs. Of the 'pot' variety a
delighted New Forest customer wrote to the maker "I am
rejoicing over the Kay pot supplied by my builder. As in
Aesop's Fable of the wind and the sun and the man's
overcoat, the wind is trying all out to make the chimney
smoke and it simply can't".
   The louvred pot, of infinite variety; 3 ring, with many
subtle variations; capped, in several forms; crowned;
hooded; with saddle top; with covered top; crowned with
four horns; with four, or eight, pockets; with horns, and
crowns, and hood; the octagon louvre; square based louvre;
the gipsy louvre; the single louvred pot; the special louvred
pot.
   The Lady Broughton pot, similar to a Bishop; the
Broughton pot. What is the origin of this name?
   The plain can and cap, capped can, ornamental capped
pot, capped moulded pot, capped pocket pot; the Scotch
can and cap.
   The bottle pot.

The round moulded pot (several varieties).

The eight pocket chimney pot, the twelve pocket roll, the ornamental pocket roll.

The barrel top, the eight pocket barrel top.

The hood top, the hooded horned can, horned can and cap, the hooded pocket pot.

The ogee pot.

The crown top, ornamental crown top, round crown top, pocket crown pot, louvred crown pot, taper crown pot, square-based crown pot (cf. the Bishop).

The rook.

The round vent pot.

The castle = an ornamental round pot, with spiral ornamentation and battlemented top.

The moulded—fluted, round—spiked top.

The Venetian = the Sankey pot, the improved Sankey. This makes claim to be invaluable in coastal areas. 'Everyone is familar with this artistic and efficient chimney-pot'. It bears no resemblance to any chimney in Venice.

The Georgian = The Guardian = the Smokecure = the 123 (Ensor). This boasts of Royal Patronage, being used on Buckingham Palace, and (much more conspicuously) on St. James' Palace. 'Hundreds of Tallboys have been replaced with pots of this design', Red Bank, 1966.

The Marcone—with a very long hat.

The Smokecure (ii) = the Spiral vent = Wilson's Patent Ventilating Spiral Chimney-Pot (1845) "for the cure of smoky chimneys is the only article for the purpose which assists the draught of the chimney by an external propelling power. Upwards of 50 were fixed last winter on the chimneys of Buckingham Palace and Windsor Castle with great success. This chimney-pot is not only the best and most effectual ever invented for the purpose named, but stands

unrivalled in its ornamental appearance. The public may be
supplied with the above useful article by any of the
respectable ironmongers". etc.

The horned pot; two horned, four horned; two horned
roll, two horned hooded.

The horned crowned pot.

The horned hooded pot.

The Irish roll pot.

The London roll pot.

The Mushroom top.

The Venturi.

The Supira. This last-named, a square louvred contrivance, looks the latest thing in chimney-pots. It has found
its way all over Britain and France. It has several
varieties. 'Eliminates down-draught and blow-back. Ensures
constant regular draught whatever the wind or weather'.

The 'Baffler', Oakes patent no. 16140, and bearing an
oak leaf trade-mark. There are some strange chimney-pots
after this pattern in the main street of Steyning, Sussex.

The H-pot: or "O-H".

The Airex (Ensor).

The Norris (ditto). Both these last, exaggerated forms of
the Bishop.

The Robertson pot (ditto), with projecting louvre and
cap: round or square. "Well in advance of any other type
on the market. Has an exceptionally powerful exhaust capacity which prevents down-draught and makes a fire burn
cleanly and brightly. Will draw air from a chimney with the
wind blowing vertically down from it".

The Southport pot and the Register pot are specialities
of Cumberworth; this works also produces a special tallboy,
the top half of which is fluted. This last-named chimney-
pot is common in the Huddersfield-Halifax region.

A Scottish list (Messrs. Loudoun and Russell, Newmains) consists of the following cans. Single beaded can, common can and cap, horned can and cap, octagon can, Dublin can, Emperor can, Horned Emperor, Tubed Emperor, Louvre can and cap, Horned or tubed caps, wind-guard octagon can, single barrel can, crescent can, double barrel or T-can, Rainproof top (resembling a lighthouse), Loudoun's patent (octagonal top), scalloped can, square leaf can, and the Champion.

None of these makers in their catalogue include the giant London or Reading tallboys, some of these as high as seven and a half feet, and used to save the building of a higher chimney-stack; the tapering red pots of Regency Bath or Brighton; the handsome terra cotta pots of the Chichester area (see the last chapter), or the old pots seen about York and in a number of places in the north-east, or the large black glazed ringed pots used by the railways on thousands of their buildings in the last century. No mention is made of the 'Fareham reds' which until recently had a market over much of the south and south-west of England.

As there is a wide variety of chimney-pots still extant, and in most cases still being manufactured, so there is an infinite variety, in every area, of selection and arrangement of chimney-pots, from the short stack with one flue terminal to a long stack with twenty or more different pots or cowls on it. Someone has written that "there is a gay impudence about some congregations of chimney-pots that can be rather endearing". But he goes on "Usually the pot is an excrescence. Apart perhaps from a tangle of Television aerials, nothing can do more to destroy the grace of a skyline than a prominent assemblage of pots and cowls, and I suspect that there are many people who may not have realised that they could improve the appearance of their house by asking a builder to sink or remove these anomalous objects." Needless to say, we do not agree with these sentiments!

Many chimney-pots are designed for their aesthetic effect: this is specially true of the kind that are miniature imitations of Tudor chimneys, and of the square and octagonal varieties. As we have seen, there are many handsome Georgian pots extant.

If we would seek unity of design in a street, we have only to look at many parts of London, at the back streets of any northern industrial town, at the Georgian parts of Edinburgh, Brighton, and Bath, with their long chimney stacks with armies of pots, reposing restfully on the roofs. The buildings of Portsmouth dockyard are nearly all surmounted by tallboys crowned with primitive lobster-backs; the old High Street in Fareham boasts a number of identical milk-can chimney-pots. Unity of design in chimneys may be seen in a street of bungalows in Edinburgh or Dundee, with their tall square chimneys on either side.

But it is the differences, not the similarities, which make for interest. Among towns through which it is a delight to stroll gazing at the chimneys are Salisbury, Cambridge, Blandford, Kendal, Chichester, Fareham, Skipton, Windsor, Steyning, Petersfield, Saffron Walden, Wakefield, Marlow, Stamford, Lyme Regis, Montrose, Arbroath, Wimborne, Wareham, Stow on the Wold and Hungerford. Of these Kendal is the most remarkable. Too many towns have lost valuable old chimneys by enemy action or by ordinary demolition, especially Canterbury, Portsmouth, Dundee, and Oxford.

Among villages with the most delightful chimneyscapes may be selected the following: Milnthorpe in Westmorland, Chawton in Hampshire, Biddenden in Kent, Selworthy in

Somerset, Tollard Royal in Wiltshire, Burwash in East
Sussex, Funtington in West Sussex, Corfe Castle in Dorset,
Puddletown in the same county, Stanton in Gloucestershire,
Ivinghoe in Buckinghamshire, Broadway in Worcestershire,
Albury in Surrey, Dorchester on Thames in Oxfordshire,
Fingest (plate 34) and Brill in Buckinghamshire, and Great
Sampford in Essex. Alderminster (Warwickshire) and Nune-
ham Courtenay (Oxfordshire) provide uniform chimneyscapes
arising out of an estate pattern for their respective villages.
Corfe is the finest of them all, with its lovely Purbeck
stone and red brick stacks, and variety of typical Dorset and
Wiltshire chimney tops.

He would be a dull man who did not admit there
is not a little humour to be found in pot design. What
one might call 'Strawberry Hill Gothick' chimney-pots are
quaint enough. But among the louvred, horned, spiked
and hooded varieties there is more often than not what
one writer previously quoted called a whimsical effect.
The National Clayware Federation's official catalogue shows
some strangely quaint contrivances—a richly ornamented
tapering pot with a richly ornamented hat; the H-pot or
Tee-can which always looks funny; a tee-can lavishly
sprouted below the top; a spirally ornamented pot with a
battlemented top; a lighthouse; a closed tulip; a squinched
octagon covered with louvres and a hood; a snarling beast
with nostrils breathing fire; two square pots with richly
ornamented panels and bizarre spiking at the top; an Early
English pillar with six lancet windows in it; while it is
also possible to see in the same catalogue a mini-coat, a man
at 'arms bend', and a pair of binoculars. The designers of
many of these had a touch of the art of Gaudi in them.
Nor is anyone likely to forget Robert Stephen Hawker's
eccentricities at Morwenstow, where he had the vicarage

chimneys built as replicas of the towers of Morwenstow and North Tamerton church towers, Magdalen Tower in Oxford, and his mother's tomb. I have also heard of a strange set of chimneys in Colinton Road, Edinburgh, ordered to be made in the shape of pen-nibs by a pen-manufacturer famous for the widely-known rhyme advertising his wares :

"They come as a boon and a blessing to men.
The Pickwick, the Owl and the Waverley pen".

These three famous pens are immortalized in their chimney.

Even more noticeable are the odd and humourous effects of arrangements or combinations of chimney-pots. "The horse's head" is suggested by a stack on one gable only of a two gabled house. It is easy to interpret certain common chimney-pot arrangements as 'Baby's first teeth', 'Gap toothed', 'Teeth missing', 'Ears cocked up', 'Front and Back Studs', and 'three-pronged fork', 'the twelve Apostles'; or as 'Clean bowled', 'Middle Stump Uprooted', 'Head and Shoulders', 'Stand at Ease' (of a chimney with two external flues), 'Leaning Drunkenly'; while the Wilts and Dorset four-pillars-surmounted-by-a-slate arrangement can be called a table top, and a lobster-back can resemble a sitting cat.

It is possible even to see expressions on pots or arrangements of them; benign, evil, nonchalant, complacent, cosy.

Mrs. E. A. Jacob in *Pots and Personalities or High Life in London* (London, de la More Press), saw in the complex cowls of London 'an old man with a beard;' 'Two's company, three's none'; 'Love's young dream'; 'An angry father—what do you mean by it?'; 'Scandal—three old cats'; 'The first walk'; 'Going to church'; 'The verger'; 'The tedious sermon' (one nearby pot to many further ones); 'Hyde Park orator' (a similar arrangement); 'H. M.'s Levee'; and 'Goodbye'. Others have seen 'Straw-hatted men', 'Kings standing afar off not amused', and 'Young Men wearing trilbies' (Mrs. E. Barraclough in *The York-shire Dalesman* of July 1962).

In a more serious mood, a church monthly recently had as its frontispiece a London rooftop scene, showing multitudes of chimney-pots, with the caption, 'Loneliness?' One could add, Over-crowding, squalor, no fuel, no sani-tation?

D.

A word or two must be said about chimney-cowls. The word cowl comes from the Latin cucullus, a hood. Percy L. Marks (op. cit.) says that cowls are "apt to be very unsatisfactory". The principle of a veering or re-volving cowl is to catch the prevailing wind and by its pulling action to cause an up-draught in the chimney. But, he says, a cowl can only be employed advantageously when a constant air current can be obtained. Cowls are too often ineffective through their liability to clog and rust, and through their weakness of mechanism. You see very many which are not working. Cowls should not be necessary, and their very existence proves the chimney imperfect.

The commonest cowl is probably the H cowl, and its near kinsman the 'donkey-leg'; there are ready-made chimney-pots in these shapes, but the metal varieties must be classed as cowls. In 1965 a metal cowl of this shape cost 103/-, and a pot version of the same 128/6. It is advertised as "the certain cure for down-draught in chimneys. Whatever the weather, an O.H. pot or cowl will rid your rooms of smoke and fumes". With it goes a guarantee that "should it fail to give satisfaction within three months of purchase, the cost of the pot or cowl plus builder's erecting charges will be refunded without question". Of it an enthusiastic householder writes "It is amazing to see the smoke emitting from the four openings, especially at times when it literally pours out of the two bottom ones, and not a trace of smoke coming into the room". Almost equally common is the lobster-back, a quarter-circle surmounted usually by an arrow (plate 24). Marks is scathing about this well-known device. "The lobster-back", he says, "holds the smoke temporarily at the top, and thus draws the air upwards by suction through the flue, in this way repelling down-draught. But the unreliability of the lobster-back and other cowls is but too well-known; when gusts of wind occur in more or less rapid succession, the action of the cowl is so erratic as to allow the wind being driven down into the flue". There are three forms of lobster-back. A simple almost triangular cowl, which can be seen in large numbers at Portsmouth Dockyard, is common also in France; the common lobster-back has already been referred to; and there is a very much larger one, bizarre in effect, which can be seen rarely in England and in other countries. The helmet cowl, which spins round so fast and is known in Scotland as a 'Granny', is a notable feature in Britain's chimneyscape. You can see hundreds of them in an Edinburgh street; few 'buts and bens' with one or two pots at each end are without at least one 'Granny'.

The small 'Chinese hat' that surmounts so many chimneys as a spark arrestor and rain preventer is such a simple contrivance that it can hardly be called a cowl. The well known comparatively modern Colt-cowl does not move; its slats are intended for the same purpose as the openings in such a chimney pot as the 'Guardian'.

Perhaps the most interesting of all cowls, to look at, are the now rare revolving cowls which resemble an old-

PLATE 1

Abingdon Abbey.

13th-century chimney stack.

*Note additional
contemporary opening
for smoke from wine-cellar
chimney, on left.*

PLATE 2

Bayeux.

La Lanterne des Morts.

PLATE 3 *Kingham, Oxfordshire. 13th-century chimney on old Manor House.*

PLATE 4 *Abingdon Abbey. 15th-century chimney-shafts (restored).*

PLATE 5

Castle Cottage,
Great Bedwyn, Wiltshire.
15th-century chimney.

PLATE 6

The chimneys of
Chambord, France.
Late 16th century.

PLATE 7

*East Barsham
Manor, Norfolk.*
*Tudor
chimney stack.*

PLATE 8
East Barsham Manor.
Detail.

PLATE 9
Lavenham, Suffolk.
16th-century chimney-stack.

PLATE 10

Lichfield, Staffordshire.
16th-century
almshouse chimneys.

PLATE 11

Woodyates Inn, Dorset.
Late 17th-century arcaded
stack (now demolished).

PLATE 12
The Pavilion, Brighton, Sussex.
Eccentric chimneys.

PLATE 13
Chichester pots.   St. Pancras.
Early 19th century.   Single band and thumb moulding.

PLATE 14

Chichester pots.
Franklyn Place.
Regency.
Triple band and plain orange pots.

LATE 15
ontwell, Sussex.
robably early 19th century.
ale orange.
ossibly unique design.

PLATE 16   *Chichester, Franklyn Place.*
Regency.   Some rare pots.   All orange, the perforated pot the deepest colour.

PLATE 17   *Chichester, South Pallant.   A fine selection of unusual pots.   All orange.*

PLATE 18   *Chichester, Franklyn Place.   Regency.   All orange.*
Neither specimen has the stippled band seen below the thumb moulding on the central pot shown in plate 13.

PLATE 19   *Chichester, Franklyn Place.   Regency.   A variety of periods and designs.*

PLATE 20
Chichester, Franklyn Place.
Regency.
A treble improvisation! All orange.

PLATE 21
Chichester, East Pallant.
Probably mid-18th century.
An orange pot showing rare slip design.

PLATE 22
Chichester, St. Pancras.
Possibly mid-18th century.
A dark red pot
with double band of slip.

PLATE 23

London.
18th-century
stack and pots.

PLATE 24
Tredington, Warwickshire.
A 'lobster back'.

PLATE 25   London, Southwark.   18th-century pots.

PLATE 26 *A 'Supira' pot (centre) near Stow on the Wold.*

PLATE 27 *Brighton, Sussex. Some eccentric cowls.*

PLATE 28

Regional chimneys.
Left: Lakeland, South Devon and Dartmoor.
Right: Exmoor, Herefordshire and the Cotswolds.

PLATE 29

London, Southwark.
An Italianate
factory chimney.

PLATE 30

The Lakeland 'tent' style
on the left.

On the right, the flat slab
and stone device,
showing the open corners
just below the slab.

PLATE 31 *A composite Lakeland stack with the two-slate 'tent'.*

PLATE 32 *Broadway, Worcestershire. A two-pillared stone chimney.*

PLATE 33

Lichfield.

16th-century almshouse chimney of Midland 'star' design.

PLATE 34

Fingest, Buckinghamshire.

An original stack and cover.

PLATE 35
Wiltshire 'table-tops'
at Tollard Royal.

PLATE 36
The crooked stack of
the Chichester area.
(House now demolished.)
18th century.

PLATE 37 *Chichester, Franklyn Place. Regency varieties.*

PLATE 38 *Dedham, Essex. Pillared chimney stacks.*

PLATE 39   *East Anglian farmhouse chimneys at Stratford St. Mary.*

PLATE 40   *Near Ballybunion, Kerry: the low chimney stacks of the Irish 'cabin'.*

fashioned church stove. These are rapidly becoming museum pieces. They should be carefully observed, in their taller or shorter forms. Spiral iron cowls, which certainly existed in Chichester forty years ago, seem to have disappeared. A tin cowl seen in Sixpenny Handley, Dorset, recently, would seem to be unique. It is a straight iron cylinder which mushrooms out into a much larger cylinder, with frills at the top and bottom.

Finally, no mention of cowls can be made without reference to Brighton, where the largest selection of oddly shaped cowls in the country can still be seen. A feature of these is that while many follow conventional patterns, nearly all have their stems bent (plate 27).

Interesting cowls lead a precarious existence: it is all too possible to note their interest one day, and at one's next visit to find them gone. Cowls repay a careful study, and the study could well be extended to their cousins, the various kinds of ridge and roof ventilators.

E

Chapter Four

REGIONAL VARIETIES OF CHIMNEYS IN GREAT BRITAIN

Every district of Great Britain has its own regional specialities so far as chimneys and chimney-pots are concerned. I refer to vernacular chimneys and pots, with vernacular architecture. It is impossible to reckon with all the common modern chimney-pots, which while also assignable to regions in many cases, are not sufficiently interesting or beautiful to include in this section. Specialization in chimney architecture or the use of chimney-pots varies in many regions of Great Britain; some regions like that round Chichester and Fareham being very small, others being as big as Scotland, in the length and breadth of which there is little variation of chimney usage. Regional uses do however cut across one another, it being possible to see a speciality of one region cropping up in a quite different region.

We will start with the region which has probably the most striking chimney arrangements of all in Great Britain —the Lake District. Here the chimneys drew forth the admiration of William Wordsworth. In his *Guide to the Lake District* Wordsworth says "Nor will the singular beauty of the chimneys escape the eye of the attentive traveller. Sometimes a low chimney, almost upon a level with the roof, is overlaid with a slate, supported upon four slender pillars. Others are of a quadrangular shape, rising

one or two feet above the roof; which low square is
often surmounted by a tall cylinder, giving to the cottage
chimney the most beautiful shape in which it is ever seen
(plate 28). Nor will it be too fanciful or refined to remark,
that there is a pleasing harmony between a tall chimney of
this circular form, and the living column of smoke, ascending from it through the still air." With Wordsworth's
four slender pillars surmounted by a slate, we may compare
the chimneys (of brick) of this kind which we have noted
in Wiltshire and Dorset and eastward in the Weald of
Sussex and Kent. With his tall cylinder we may compare
the North Devon and Somerset round chimneys. One of
the loveliest sights in the Lake District and in the Kendal-
Sedbergh-Kirkby Lonsdale district is the old 'statesman's'
farmhouse with its tall cylindrical chimneys at the two
gable-ends—and a third bringing up the rear from a
cross-gable—all surrounded by trees and backed by the
dark fell side. Wordsworth does not mention the fact that
many Lakeland chimneys are corbelled out high up in the
wall: or that some are buttressed or stepped. He says
nothing of the two commonest Lakeland devices: four
slates peaked at the tops, surmounted by a slate and kept
in position by a big stone (plate 30); and two slanting
slates meeting together over the chimney-hole. The first
of these can be compared with a primitive 'chimney-pot'
made of a square of four slates, each one peaked at the top:
this may be seen all down the middle west of England, to
Oxford (where there are many examples, on older houses)
and beyond. The second is a common chimney-device in
Somerset, Devon, and Cornwall; and in central France.
Wordsworth of course wrote before the coming of the
glazed chimney-pot to the lake District. It has, in comparatively recent years, blossomed with the products of

the Northern chimney-pot factories. Beatrix Potter made very little of these endearing Lake District landmarks. She shows mainly plain stacks, though she draws a strange chimney in 'Jemima Puddle Duck' (page 28) and shows Lake District chimney devices on page 58 of the same book. We have already observed that Kendal is probably Britain's finest town for good chimneyscapes.

The stone areas of Yorkshire, Lancashire, and Derbyshire are characterized by modest solid stacks with good copings, and baked fireclay chimney-pots. A stunted louvred pot, a Bishop, a louvred Bishop, and a taller louvred pot with outward-looking spikes, are all characteristic of this district, while throughout the north a square tapering flue-terminal is very common. We shall notice prominent stacks with proud arrays of these more florid pots on the homes of West Riding industrialists; and often the most handsome assemblage of stacks and pots in the streets of Weavers' cottages that still characterize many northern towns. Splendid seventeenth-century stepped and buttressed chimneys may be seen from Halifax in the West Riding to Coxwold in the East Riding : the last named village has a notable stepped chimney at Lawrence Sterne's 'Shandy Hall'.

The Cotswolds, and the limestone belt in general are notable for fine and sturdy, yet graceful, chimney-stacks; "lofty well-designed chimney-stacks crowned with generous cornices" (Clifton Taylor, op. cit.). Many stacks are double —each flue having its independent chimney-shaft—and are joined by the cornice at the top, sharing also a solid base (plate 32). There is sparing use of chimney-pots in this area, for the chimney-stacks here are such that pots might really look incongruous : such pots as there are are less conspicuous because of the size and status of the stacks. A yellow pot, with a spiky crown over little holes which help to let out the smoke, is perhaps the most popular in this area. The square spiked pot is almost as common (plate 32). The great mansion of Sezincote has copper chimney-pots. At Snowshill is a cottage with a projecting bread oven adjoining one of its chimneys.

In the Midland clay belt one notices chiefly the plain brick stacks, often very tall, bearing buff or red pots. These are mainly gable stacks. The predominant chimney-pots are the Bishop and the square pot. The Bishop may be red, buff or of burnt fireclay : the square pot is, as often as, not, spiked at the four corners (plate 32). A speciality of this area is the star-shaped stack (plate 33). In East Anglia chimneys became general about the year 1450. One should notice the many cottages with steep roofs and one axial chimney-stack; the tall and slender chimney-stacks of the Norfolk houses; the old black pots of Norfolk; the central chimney stacks lying along, not at right angles to, the ridge of the roof; and the predominating use, especially in Suffolk, of stacks without any pots. Buckinghamshire's specialities are splendid old brickwork chimney-stacks; and an ogival hood for the top of chimney-pots. The Reading area is notable, as we have already observed, for fine rust-red pots and many tallboys of outsize dimensions. Through Wiltshire and Dorset one comes frequently across the 'table top' type of chimney top (plate 35). Above the coping of a simple brick stack rise four pillars of brick at the four corners, supporting a slate as rain excluder or spark arrestor. In its spark-arresting capacity this device (or some variant of it) is very common in thatched houses and cottages. In these counties are splendid examples of the 'tea-caddy' stack, usually 17th or 18th century. Kent and Eastern Sussex specialize in the magnificent chimney stacks

of wealden farmhouses and cottages, already referred to.
West Sussex and Hampshire come under the influence of
Fareham. In this town, to the present day, potteries have
made fine chimney-pots, and everywhere from round Chichester to Winchester and Salisbury (Mompesson House has
some) you may see the proud Fareham Reds, banded near
the top with white ornamentation. This is perhaps the
handsomest chimney-pot in Britain (plates 13, 14, 16, 22,
& 37). Also made in this area is a small slug pellet type
of pot which looks as if it had been overpainted white
on red or black and bears the marks of the potter's wheel.
Many examples of it can still be seen at Funtington in West
Sussex. We have already spoken of the strange crooked
chimney-stacks of the Chichester area. One curiosity
still deserves attention. It is a tapering stuccoed cylinder
surmounting the chimney stack. It is an early kind of 'pot',
yet can sometimes be seen carrying pots itself (there is
an example at Singleton). The finest example of this device
can be seen in the centre of Fittleworth. But, though this is
a speciality of West Sussex, we meet it again at Corfe
Castle. Much further west, Devon, Somerset and Cornwall
as we have already observed, specialize in front chimneys,
round chimneys, and while having no distinctive pots,
make very conspicuous use of the two-slate device common
in the Lake District.

Almost a separate chapter could be written about the
chimneys of Scotland. The use of the chimney-pot is there
almost universal: plain stacks without pots are rare, except
for such as survive on old castles. Chimneys which are part
of the original design of old castles can be seen at
Dirleton (built 1225), Tioram and Skipness (13th century),
Neidpath, Doune, and Craigmillar (14th century), Affleck,
Borthwick and Caerlaverock (15th century), Claypotts

(1569-88), Menzies (1571-7), and Elcho (1580). Chimneys on castles are often corbelled out, as at Crathes and Claypotts. Drumlanrig (Dumfrieshire) is almost a Scottish Chambord : its stacks are surmounted by square pots each terminating in an odd little brush-like structure. Plain buff pots are commonest in Scotland, of varying length, almost invariably crowned by a hat which looks like an inverted bucket. The pot beneath the hat is not infrequently sprouted or 'horned'. A very large proportion of buildings sport at least one revolving 'granny' or helmet cowl. Octagonal pots are common also in Scotland. Among interesting arrangements of chimneys we may note the following : the side-wall chimneys of many of the older tenement houses in big cities; and the 'gable-endie' chimneys of the East coast, crowning a cross-gable fronting the street. The setting of chimneys to finish off tall gables is a feature of Scottish domestic architecture. Often you see two gable chimneys in a rectangular house, but also one in a small gable over the front door (with a staircase window over the door); such chimneys may be dummies. Diagonally set chimneys of stone as in the Cotswolds, are rare, but there is one at Hill House, Dunfermline, and some at Innes House, Morayshire, arising straight out of the gable without a plinth. Round chimneys are to be seen in the central keep at Glamis. Buttressed chimneys can be seen at Auchanachy Castle, Aberdeenshire. Some 17th-century lairds' houses are divided into three main portions by two thick partition walls containing chimney flues whch emerge in the centre of the roof, as at Airds House, Argyll; Lochlane and Glendoick, Perthshire. Ornamental octagonal chimneys surmount two cupola'd towers at Duff House, Banffshire, built by Adam in 1730-40. At Mavisbank, Midlothian, the whole front elevation of the roof is surmounted by a length

of chimney stack showing 18 pots in a row. In some of the
streets and squares of Georgian Edinburgh great transverse
stacks may be observed, with each a single line of over 20
pots in a row. Many large Scottish houses have a forest
of chimneys rising from the roof of the central block;
sometimes eight stacks, two looking in each direction. Pillar
chimneys in pairs or more are to be found at Culzean
Castle, Ayrshire (built by Adam, 1771-1792), and Dun-
ninald Castle, Angus (1819-32).

A word should be said about the chimneys of ancient
black-houses and long houses. The black house—and some
of them still survive—had a stone hearth near the middle
of the kitchen floor; the smoke drifted upwards through
the thatch, or found its way through a smokehole placed
a little to one side of the fire. Long houses had the fire
in the centre of the kitchen, the smoke being gathered into
a wide canopied chimney of wattle-and-daub or lath-and-
plaster, which, suspended over the fire and reaching to
within five feet of the ground, looked like an inverted
funnel. An 18th-century drawing of 'An Inn in Ross-shire'
shows a hole in the thatch for letting out the smoke. In
many of these old homesteads today a chimney-pot is
inserted into the thatch; at Bernisdale, Skye, is an actual
chimney of thatch.

We must not overlook the fact that regional uses in
chimneys and chimney-pots cut across one another, and
even have their counterpart abroad. The chimney devices of
the Lake District show a remarkable similarity to some
in the mountain-valleys of Ticino, and to others at Albe-
robello (the town of trulli) in Southern Italy. The table-
tops of Wiltshire and Dorset have not only spilled over into
Sussex and Kent but the same device is the most popular
chimney-top in many parts of central Europe—especially

in the Black Forest. The stone stacks of the Cotswolds and of other English limestone districts bear a resemblance to the chimneys of the Bocage district of Normandy. The Normandy long house has a smaller central stack than the almost identical use in Wiltshire, Dorset and Devon. The two sloped tiles covering the smoke hole in the Lake District and in the south-west of England can be met again in Central France; here the tiles are in many cases ornamented, and they are often joined by a coping. Round chimney-stacks are common to the Lake District and to North Devon and Somerset..

Chapter Five

CHIMNEYS IN OTHER LANDS

We finished the last chapter in Scotland, where it must not be forgotten that a chimney is called a 'lum'. What is it called in other lands? In Greece the kapnodoke of ancient Greek has given way to Kapnodoche in modern Greek, but the modern Greek calls it also kaminada, or fougaro. The Latin caminus has become camino in Italian. French cheminée and Spanish chimenea are similar. The Rumanian word is cos. Modern Gaelic has simne, and Welsh simdde or simnai. In Norwegian it is reykberi, reykhafr, or skorsteiner; this last word has its counterparts in the Danish and Swedish skorsten, the Dutch schoorsteen, and the Old, Middle, and New High German with scorenstein, schorstein, and schormstein respectively. Modern German also uses the words kamin, and rauchfang. Latvian for chimney is skurstenis. We return to something like the Latin caminus in the Lithuanian kaminas, the Bohemian and the Polish komin. The Russians call a chimney truba, and the Serbo-Croatian word is dimnjak or odzak.

In Eire one notes an almost universal use of mere flue-terminals, round and squat. There is in fact in that country an utter economy over chimney-pots. Apart from the ubiquitous flue-terminal, one notices just a few octagonal pots, and a fair number of Irish Rolls and Dublin cans; occasionally one meets a lobster-back. Eire is sparing, too, over chimney-stacks (pl. 40). The stack barely rises

above the roof or gable, and is seldom—and then only mod-
estly—corniced. We spoke of regional specialities overlapping.
I have seen two English Midland square spiked pots on
a cottage in a lonely road in County Kerry! It can be
conjectured that pots came fairly late to Ireland. Hall's
Ireland (1841) shows pots in Cork and Dublin: but very
few—pots were very rare at that date. The same work
gives evidence of the existence at that date of wicker
chimneys in old cottages. It is still possible to see, in
the older thatched cabins, a pot stuck in the thatch to
serve as a chimney, as we saw in the 'Black houses' of
the Western Isles of Scotland.

France could be said to go in for chimney-pots to a
greater degree than any land except Great Britain
(Figs 1, 2 & 3). But France's stacks are thin and spare,
and her pots miniature (Fig. 1)—in some cases a miniature
version of British pots and cowls. One sees few ancient
chimney pots in France, and though evidence is hard
to obtain, France does not seem to have used chimney-
pots before they were used widely (during the 18th century)
in Britain. A Corot painting (1833) of the Ile de la Cité
in Paris shows all kinds of chimneys and chimney-pots,
and includes actually a lobster-back. France's most popular
chimney-pot is a short squinched affair, nearly always red.
There are also taller versions of this pot, and one which ends in
a lighthouse top (Fig. 1, no. 5). The smaller of these pots are
often surmounted by a tall cylinder of tin, to the top of
which is fitted a 'Chinese hat' (Fig. 1, no. 3). In Normandy
and the north, stacks and pots and their arrangements
approach the English styles: but one notices the flimsier
stacks, and the half-size pots, although the proportions
look right enough. The four-pillars-covered-by-a-slate
chimney top is common in France, though the slate often

CHIMNEYS OF FRANCE

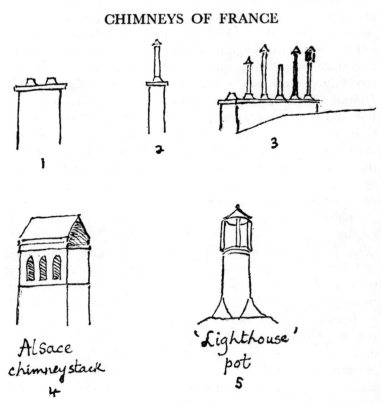

Fig. 1

overlaps as it does not in England. The Lake District or North Devon two-tile arrangement can be seen frequently in France; in Central France these tiles are in many cases ornamented. We note nearer Germany and Switzerland the extensive use of a gabled chimney, with three lancet-like openings at each side beneath the 'roof'. This chimney is common in Alsace (Fig. 1, no. 4), but it may be found in many other parts of France. I have seen one of these,

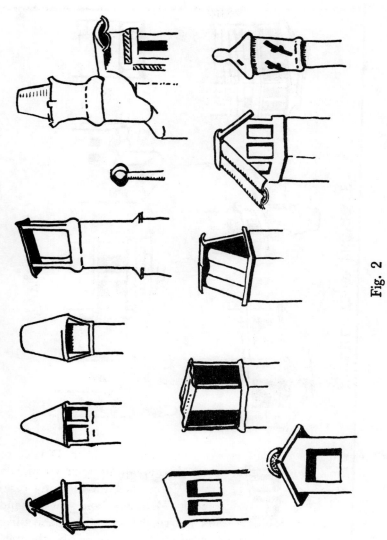

Fig. 2

77

CHIMNEYS OF PROVENCE

Fig. 3

at Remiremont in Alsace, surmounted by a large wrought iron weathercock.

We have already seen something of the history of chimneys and chimney-pots in Italy from studying early Italian paintings. Though chimneys are small in Italy and masked, and play little or no part in a town or village skyline, they are nevertheless highly picturesque and beautiful in design (Fig. 4). They are usually hardly visible from the street, but there are plenty visible from the air or from any higher vantage point. A very occasional pot may be seen; white, medium height, with a bulbous top; tall and thin, of sheet metal, with a 'Chinese hat'; red and ending in a lighthouse top. Our line-drawing illustration shows the most attractive and conspicuous types of chimney. Samuel Butler, in his *Alps and Sanctuaries,* had an eye for them, and some of our drawings are after the illustrations in that book. It goes without saying that the chimneys of Venice[2] are among the most beautiful, and ought to be the most famous, in the world—these shapely, funnel-like structures often have a considerable amount of ornamentation, on the stack itself, at the neck, and on the projecting funnel.

The towns and villages of the Netherlands have their skylines well serrated with plenty of chimneys, but all are small and inconspicuous. We know the vernacular chimneys of these countries well, through studying the masters of Flemish and Dutch landscape-painting. We know that chimney-pots have been in use in the Netherlands from the sixteenth century. No artist depicts any interesting chimneys or pots save G. Berckheyde (1638-98) who shows corniced stacks and one with a roof of its own. An Arnhem

[2] That Italy had chimneys at least before 1347 can be seen from a record left of several chimneys being demolished by an earthquake in Venice in 1347. In the 1370 decade the Italian type of chimney was brought to England.

CHIMNEYS OF ITALY

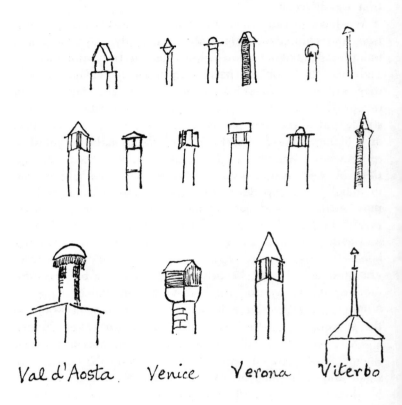

Val d'Aosta   Venice   Verona   Viterbo

Fig. 4

correspondent writes thus of Dutch chimneys today. "Chimney flues are always laid in small yellow bricks, and the upper part of the chimney in red or yellow bricks. Many times they are covered with a flat or curved iron plate, to prevent rain or snow falling down". He adds that in Belgium there are no special pots, but a

kitchen-pot deprived of its bottom; "in our modern time
the use of brown glazed chimney-pipes is very common.
The tubes are much like those used for sewers or drains".
In Luxembourg today the commonest chimney arrangement is the table-top (see on Wiltshire and Dorset, and on
France). This is usually very small, but it sometimes appears
with a projecting cornice, as well as with a projecting slate
on top : sometimes it appears with more than one tile
on top, the tiles being gathered up to a peak in steps.
This little country makes use of H-pots and cowls, and
of lobster-backs. It also shows a chimney with an arched
top, the arch being corbelled out from the necking of the
chimney so that it can protect the whole stack as well as
the flue-hole. In Germany the 'table-top' variety of chimney is almost universal, and can be found in plentiful
numbers from north to south, sometimes larger, sometimes
smaller, sometimes in multiples of as many as four or six.
Gable tops are common also. But on the whole in this
country chimneys are small and inconspicuous.

The impression we get from looking at the chimneyscape
of a typical Austrian town or village (Fig. 5) is that
there is no attempt whatever made to group the chimneys
of a house. They sprout from the roofs from wherever
they are needed. Feldkirch, to take one example, shows
a forest of such chimneys. In Vienna the stacks are more
ample in size; pots, including very thin tallboys, are used
here, together with cowls and all manner of chimney tops—
including the ogival one previously remarked in Buckinghamshire. Salzburg has very small chimneys. The gable top
mentioned under 'Alsace' is commonest of all in Western
Austria, but up in the mountains the table-top is most
frequent. The Bregenzerwald shows a variety of this with a
very large projecting slate on top. Modern housing estates

F

CHIMNEYS OF AUSTRIA

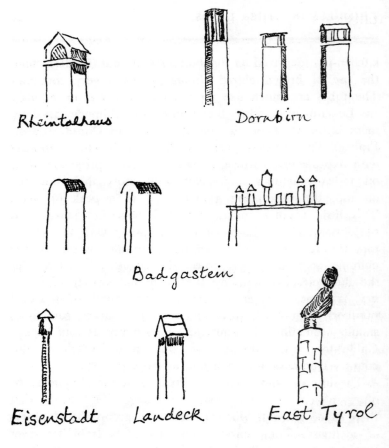

Rheintalhaus

Dorabirn

Badgastein

Eisenstadt

Landeck

East Tyrol

Rust

Fig. 5

82

in Austria have retained the vernacular styles of chimney.
Switzerland shares the best chimneys with all its near
neighbours. In Lausanne, for example, every kind of chimney can be seen; tallboys, gables, table-tops, H-pots or
cowls, and rows of tin 'pots'. In Zermatt are gables, chimney tops with pyramidal heads, various kinds of modest
chimney-pots, and a lobster-back. The Ticino has, obviously, Italian chimneys; but the rough stone houses of
the mountain valleys have chimney devices which bear
a remarkably close resemblance to those of the English
Lake District. A well known view of Lugano, looking to
Monte San Salvatore, has for its foreground roofs with
six prominent 'table-top' chimneys. Alpine huts have no
chimneys, though some sport a tin pot crowned with a
'Chinese hat'.

In Yugoslavia chimneys are sparse. The gable type is
commonest, with a variety which has a hole in the top of
the gable. There are many Venetian funnels; and plenty of
round stacks with round chimney-tops and sharp pyramidal
peaks over all. Some weird types of lobster-back appear in
this country.

In Czechoslovakia the old towns have splendid chimneyscapes. Prague has many corniced plain stacks; many
corniced, with a narrowing projection above the cornices.
It has many pots, all heavily flanged; and numerous
examples of the two slanting tiles arrangement noted
already in S.W. England and the Lake District—but these
examples in Prague are ornamented by a ridge decoration.
The country generally has plenty of variety of pots and
cowls; tall pots with hats on; gabled stacks with openings
below the gable and at the sides; chimney tops as in
the Black Forest; and an occasional lobster-back. Wooden
huts in the Carpathians have no chimneys.

In Scandinavia pots are rare, though we have seen plain drain-pipe pots, pots with long hats; tall tin pots with Chinese hats on, and primitive lobster-backs. But on the whole, it is the stacks one notices in Scandinavia. Chimney stacks, taking them by and large, are small and out of proportion to the buildings they surmount. The semi-circular hood, often of ironwork, is common. A number of old chimneys survive; most of them plain stone chimneys, usually on the ridge of a gable. Two interesting chimney features of Scandinavia are (1) the tea-caddies with ornamented panels, examples of which can be seen from Dyrehaven in Denmark to Trondheim in Norway (some of these are octagonal); and (2) the widespread practice of placing all external chimney stacks on the ridge of the roof, so that a large or long building displays quite a fine row of them. Many fine stacks exist throughout Scandinavia consisting of a plinth above roof level, a thinner stack of medium height (not infrequently ornamented) and a coping which slightly oversails. There are some fine clustered, cruciform, brick chimney-stacks in the old parts of Copenhagen. The greatest curiosity I have been able to unearth from Scandinavia is depicted in T. Paulsson's *Scandinavian Architecture* (London, 1958), where a Morastuga (South Scandinavian peasant's house with no upper storey) is shown with a very tall chimney, consisting of a low 'table top' surmounted by a very tall round pillar: this in turn has vent-holes near the top, and is finished with a bulbous head and decorated finial.

When we look at the chimneyscape of the U.S.A., or of its more or less vernacular architecture, we find several specimens that have already become familiar to us. The earlies settlers went in for the axial stack common in 17th-century English homes. This stack was often ornamented, and its use continued into the 18th century, when gable end chimneys became fairly common. From the 18th century date a number of chimneys with the 'table-top' usually in multiples of two and three and four. Examples of this are at Peekskill, Strang-Durrin house and also Springwood, Hyde Park; the Grove, Rhinebeck; and Rokeby, Barrytown. Tunnel-shaped hoods worked in brick, some peaked and some ogeed, and some in multiples of three, are common in houses of this date: as at Carters Grove and at Portsmouth, New Hampshire. The Lyman Mower house at Woodstock, Vermont, has two stacks at each gable surmounted each by a semi-circular hood, and at each end joined together by a parapet. (T. E. Lawrence's cottage near Bovington Camp in Dorset has its one chimney crowned with a peaked hood worked in tiles). Most of these 'Georgian' stacks have good cornices. Some of them have recessed arches, recessed in brick (as in some English Georgian tea-caddies: cf. Woodyates) and some have these arches hollow, the flues going up in the pillars of the arches. Many of these chimneys are painted white, with cornices of a different colour, as black or in red exposed brickwork. Some have richly ornamented cornices as the Van Cortlandt Manor House, Croton on Hudson. The Superintendent's House at West Point has four chimneys, two each in each gable, with arcading in the cornice to let out the smoke. The Governor Benning Wentworth House, at Little Harbour in New Hampshire, has stacks surmounted by roofs. Wursburg, Virginia, is a good place at which to look at beautiful stacks. The Hudson River Gothic Officers' house at West Point has stacks surmounted by four plain pillar shafts. Sunnyside, Tarrytown, almost rivals Albury, England, for its clever imitations of Tudor chimneys. The Van Reusselaer Manor House (now at

Williamstown, Mass.), a baroque mansion, has corbelled out ornamental chimneys, two at each gable, each pair joined by a balustrade.

Are chimney-pots used in the U.S.A.? Not usually at all, though in modern houses the use of plain square squat flue-terminals is widespread. Nevis, Irvington, has plain chimney-pots. Shillelagh, Fishkill, boasts one small pot. The Hendrick de Bries House, East Greenbush, has a glazed earthenware pot rising out of a gable. New Castle, Delaware, has some pots, chiefly octagonal and cream in colour. Monteigne, Natchez, surprises us with four louvred pots on a stack. Where did these come from?

We shall probably leave our chimney-hunting expeditions in the U.S.A. with an impression of many small two-gabled houses surmounted by a very modest and thin central stack having no pots. We shall meet this arrangement frequently also in Canada, as we did in Scandinavia. The Canadian stacks are particularly small and thin. Canada also shows some typical French and German arrangements, and uses a very few English-style pots.

Chapter Six

CHIMNEYS AND THE FUTURE

To a certain extent traditional chimney-stacks and chimney-pots are under sentence of death. Demolition
squads do not preserve ancient chimney-pots. Many types
of pot common in 18th- and 19th-century England are no
longer being made. Progress in the form of electric, gas,
and oil-fired heating is eliminating the necessity for the
traditional chimney. Where chimneys are having to be rebuilt, they are rebuilt with the maximum of economy. Modern
buildings, if they have chimneys, practice extreme austerity
in this department. Aesthetically, the attitude of architects
and builders to the chimney is pedestrian.

At the same time, all is change. "Traditional brickwork
flues and chimneys have given satisfactory performance
with open fires, but when new, more efficient appliances
are used in conjunction with traditional chimneys", writes
E. W. Marchant, "defects begin to appear both in the
function of the flue and in the fabric of the chimney".
Of the future of the terminal design he says: "The most
fanciful part of the whole chimney design used to be
the terminal or pot. In recent years the multifarious chimney-pot designs have fallen into disfavour and therefore
disuse. This is understandable as most of the designs had
doubtful functional claims made about them. The simple
roll around the plain chimney-pot may assist in stopping
winds causing down-draughts, but only when the wind

is blowing at a particular angle. Many possibilities exist to improve the design of terminals, both on functional and aesthetic bases—using clayware, colours, glazes and simple functional shapes are all possible. However, much work needs to be carried out before any particular type of chimney-pot can be specified for use in any particular situation. Research is required so that the parts of the whole heating system may work together and produce the correct system for a particular set of circumstances. Until then, probably, the only course to be taken is to be sure that the top of the pot is well above the line of the ridge of the roof". He informs us that research is to be initiated "into the function of terminals with particular reference to their usefulness in avoiding down-draughts and in aiding the escape of flue gases, and into their appearance".

One modern firm widely advertises round metal 'Metal-bestos' chimneys which are alleged to save space, be utterly durable, carry little weight, be easy of installation, and be usable with all kinds of fuels. These round metal chimneys can be enclosed in a synthetic 'stack' known as a 'Monterey housing' or, if for two 'pots', 'twin housing'; they terminate in a rain cap, i.e. a domed apex, or in a spark-arrestor (this being recommended for wooded areas). There are seven steps in building this chimney: Frame hole and chimney-support, fix chimney lengths, install fire-top spacers, instal joist spacer, slip on adjustable roof flashing, put on rain cap, and fasten base tee.

Kelsall and Harris, however, in speaking about the restoration of old houses, say:

"The chimney-stacks are an important part of the external elevations. If rebuilt in brick they must be generous in size and approximate to the proportions more typical of stonework than of brickwork. The common 18 inch brick stack will not do—and in any case its thin walls render the flues cold, damp, and sluggish . . . New copings to chimney-stacks should be modelled on the originals, or on examples found on local buildings of similar character and date. The design of copes varies with the locality, but the most common type found on less pretentious houses is a thin slab showing about two inches of thickness on the face and projecting not more than one and a half inches over the faces of the stack". But austerity creeps in when it comes to chimney-pots. "By the 18th century", they say, "chimney-pots had become an integral part of the design, though not such large and ornamental features as they later became in the 19th century—and replacements should be of moderate length, neither lanky nor stumpy, buff in colour and simple in form".

A strong case could be made for preservation orders on chimney-stacks and chimney-pots. It can fairly be asked, should people be allowed to demolish chimneys or take them down when necessary and rebuild them in a dull, uninteresting or disproportionate fashion?

Yet good modern chimney-stacks are still being built, especially in small villas and bungalows, many of which it seems have to have at least one large and prominent chimney built externally to the main living-room. Examples may be seen in almost any private development estate of small houses.

At least one splendid modern 'pot' is a product of the present decade. It is called the 'Supira' (plate 26) and consists of a square tiered bee-hive structure, with two, three, or more layers terminating in a peaked roof. It can be seen in many parts of France as well as in England.

Otherwise the future of chimney-stacks and pots in England looks bleak. But the same cannot be said for the future of the study of these objects. The future is bright for further study of 'Caminology', to coin a word. Many monographs could be written, as on *The Chimney-Pots of West Sussex; The Chimney-stacks of the Weald; The Chimneys of Buckinghamshire; Cotswold Chimneys; Lake District Chimney-Devices; Wessex Chimneys; The Chimney in France; Chimneys of Italy; Chimneys in Germany and Austria; New England Chimney-Stacks; In Search of Odd Chimneys.* Whole books could be written on *Chimneys Round the World,* and such titles as *A Finishing Touch to the Landscape* or *Crowning Glory* would promise a mine of interest. Moreover, the problem of who made chimney-pots before the Victorian era awaits a mountain of research.

Description of the chimneys and chimney-pots we have mentioned in this book has been difficult. But the reader has at least been introduced to a hitherto neglected subject and perhaps been shown the way for further much more specialized research. Perhaps this book should have been called *Caminology for the Beginner.* Certainly it is to be hoped that this short study will encourage him to go out looking for ancient, beautiful and interesting chimneys and that it may serve to make at least a few people active in the cause of chimney-preservation and restoration.

APPENDIX I

MODERN CHIMNEY POT DESIGNS

The publishers are indebted to the National Clayware Federation for permission to reproduce the pot designs in this appendix, the purpose of which is to provide comparisons to help the student to trace origins, and to facilitate the identification of types.

Many pots of similar design may be found in different heights, with variations in base design and measurement, etc. To list all such variations would be outside the scope of this book.

Because the illustrations which follow have been taken from a work of wider concern, the numbering of the pots illustrated is neither consecutive nor complete. The full range is nevertheless shown.

Section 1

PLAIN ROUND CHIMNEY POTS

1.	Plain Roll	26.-44. Round Pots in various sizes and designs
2.	Two Roll	
3.	Three Roll	45. Plain Round Flue Lining
4.	Dwarf Roll	46.-49. Beaded Flue Linings
5.	Broad Shouldered Roll	50, 51a. Round Pots
6.	Three Groove Roll	400. Special Roll Taper (wide base)
7.	Bottle	
8.	Irish Roll	401. Special Cannon Head
9.	Roll Base	402. Roll Taper (oval base)
10.	Beehive	403. Plain Taper
11.	Moulded Roll	404. Bellied
12.	Cannon Head	405.-406 Roll Top
13.	Beaded Cannon Head	407. Bell Top
14.	Plain Taper	408. Cannon Head
15.	Louvre Base	409. Beaded Taper
16.	Dublin Can	410. Round
17.	Bellied	411. Oval Flue Lining
18.	Flanged Cannon Head	412. Plain Taper
19.	London Roll	413.-414. Round
20.	Parallel Roll	415. Three Roll
21.	Ditto with base	416. Short Cap
22.	Two Roll with Flanged Base	417-420. Round Pots, various
23.	Curved Roll	421. Beaded Taper
24.	Plain Roll Taper	422-426. Round Pots various
25.	Moulded Roll	427-450a. Roll Tops various

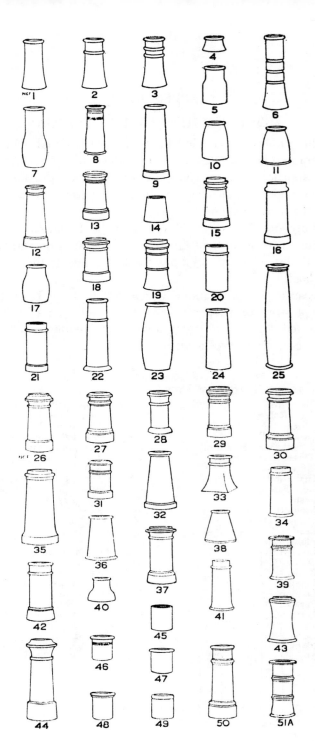

92

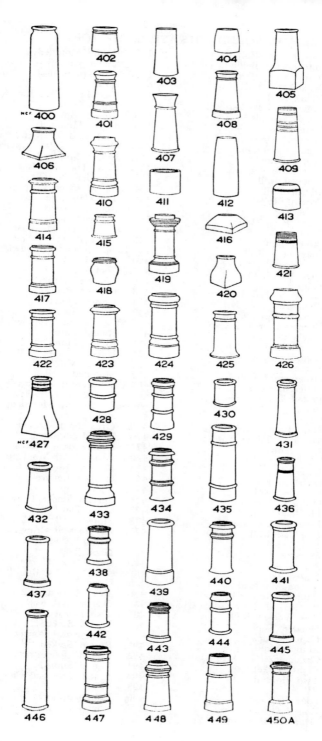

93

ORNAMENTAL ROUND POTS AND LOOSE TOPS

51. Four Pocket Roll
52. Four Pocket Bellied
53. Four Pocket Beehive
54. Ornamental Roll
55. Pocket Roll
56. Ornamental Pocket Roll
57. Round Moulded
58. Barrel Top
59-60. Round Moulded
61. Ornamental Fluted
62. Round Fluted
63. Four Ring Beehive
64. Grooved Roll
65. Ribbed Roll
66. Hooded Roll
67. Hood Top
68. Three Ring Roll
69. Cowl Top
70. Crown Top
71. Four Ring Roll
72. Ornamental Beehive
73. Four Roll Taper
74. Tulip
75. Round Spiked Top
76. Plain Can and Cap
77. Hooded Horn Can
78. Horned Can and Cap
79. Single Louvre
80. Ornamental Crown
81. Round Vent
82. Three Roll
83. Ornamental Roll
84. Fluted Beehive
85. Fluted Taper
86. Moulded Beehive
87. Capped Can
88. Four Pocket Moulded
89. Moulded Taper Pot
90. Cowl Top
91. Moulded Spiked
92. Barrel Top
93. Moulded Pocket
94. Moulded Roll
95. Capped Cam
96. Moulded Roll
97. Moulded Beehive
98. Moulded Roll
99. Moulded Beehive
100. Ornamental Capped
101. Special Round
102. Fluted Top
103. Round Moulded
104. Capped Moulded
105-109. Round Moulded, various
110. Four Pocket Roll
111. Hooded Taper
112. Capped Pocket
113. Round Moulded
114. Ornamental Beehive
115. Eight Pocket
116. Two Horned
117. 'H'
118. Four Horned
119. Round Crown Top
120. Ornamental Round

121. Round Moulded
122. Smoke Cure
123-125 Ornamental Round, various
126. Two Piece 'H', round
127. Saddle Top
128. Round Moulded
129. Taper Moulded
130-132 Moulded Round, various
133. Two Piece 'H' square base
134. Round Moulded
135. Cowl Top with Lid
136. Moulded Beehive
137-138. Moulded various
139. Tee Can with Lid
140. Round Beaded
141. Grooved Beehive
142-147. Round Moulded
148. Eight Pocket Barrel
149-150a. Round Moulded, various
450. Moulded Roll
451. Pocket Crown
452. Moulded Fluted
453. Capped Pocket
454. Crown Louvred
455. Crown Taper
456-457. Round Moulded, various
458. Round Fluted
459. Round Moulded
460. Horned Can
461. Round Moulded
462. Moulded Roll
463-464. Round Moulded, various
465. Round Four Pocket
466-467. Round Moulded, various
468. Roll Taper
469. Ornamental Round
470. Round Moulded
471. Square Base Crown
472. Ornamental Moulded
473. Round Moulded
474. Capped Louvre
475. Loose Cap
476. Special Smoke Cure
477. Cowl Top
478. Fluted Roll
479. Ornamental Crown
480. Hooded Pocket
481. Hood Top
482. Barrel Top Horned
483-484. Ornamental Roll
485. Hood Top
486. Two Horned Roll
487. Ornamental Roll
488. Two Horned Hooded
489. Round Spiked
490. Ornamental Pocket
491. Round Spiked
492. Round Hooded
493. Round Spiked
494. Scotch Can and Cap
495. 'H'
496. Round Spiked
497. Round Hooded

95

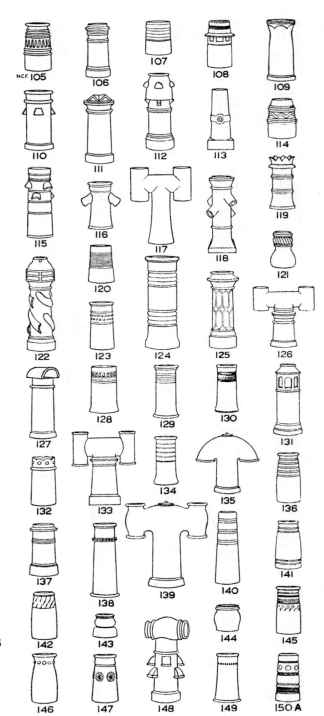

N.C.F. 105
106
107
108
109
110
111
112
113
114
115
116
117
118
119
120
121
122
123
124
125
126
127
128
129
130
131
132
133
134
135
136
137
138
139
140
141
142
143
144
145
146
147
148
149
150 A

96

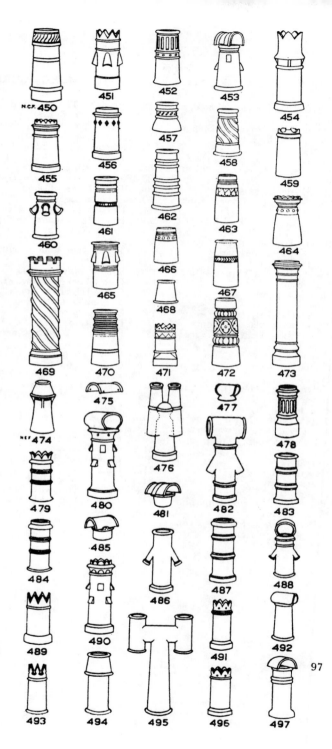

N.C.F. **450**　**451**　**452**　**453**　**454**

455　**456**　**457**　**458**　**459**

460　**461**　**462**　**463**　**464**

465　**466**　**467**

469　**470**　**468**　**471**　**472**　**473**

N.C.F. **474**　**475**　**476**　**477**　**478**

479　**480**　**481**　**482**　**483**

484　**485**　**486**　**487**　**488**

489　**490**　**491**　**492**

493　**494**　**495**　**496**　**497**

G

97

Section 3
WINDGUARDS, BISHOPS, LOUVRES AND SMOKE CURE TYPES

150. Three Ring Louvre (also four ring)
151. Three Ring Top with Spigot (also 4, 5, 6 ring)
152. Single Louvre
153. Three Ring Top without Spigot (also 4, 5, 6, 7, 8, 9, 10 ring)
154-155. Single Louvre
156. Four Pocket Three Ring Louvre
157. Loose Ring Two Lift (also 3, 4, 5, 6 Lift)
158. Eight Pocket Three Ring Louvre (also four ring)
159. Single Louvre
160. Two Piece Three Ring Louvre
161. Crown Pocket
162. Bishop
163-164 Special Louvre
165. Three Ring Capped Top
166. Three Ring Louvre, Covered Top
167. Louvre Top with Cover
168. Crown Louvre with four Horns
169. Three Ring Crown Louvre in two pieces (also 3, 4, 5, 6 ring top)
170. Three Ring Crown Louvre, one piece (also in two pieces, and 3, 4, 5, 6, 7 ring top)
171. Special Louvre
172. Capped Louvre
173. Covered Louvre
174. Special Louvre Top
175. Square Base Louvre
176. Three Ring Louvre Top (also 4, 5, 6 ring)
177. Three Ring Special Top also 4, 5, 6 ring and three ring capped)

178. Special Three Ring Top (also 4, 5, 6 ring)
179. Saddle Top Louvre, Two Lift (also 3, 4, 5, 6 lift)
180. Special Three Ring Louvre
181. Three Ring Crown Louvre
182. Three Ring Louvre
183-185. Covered Louvre Top
186. Two Piece Bishop
187. Octagon Louvre
188. Horned Louvre
189. Horned Louvre, Capped, Three Ring (also 4, 5, 6, 7 ring)
190. Three Ring Louvre with covered Top
191. Square Bishop
192. Eight Pocket Crown Louvre
193. Capped Louvre Top
194-195. Smoke Cure
196. Cone Cap
197. Dome Cap
198. Dome Cap with Spigot
199, 200. Louvre
201. Louvre Top
202. Capped Louvre
203. Eight Pocket Louvre
204. Square Base Louvre
205. Bishop
206. Louvre
207. Capped Louvre Top
208. Louvre
209. Hood Top
210. Special Louvre
211. Crown Top Louvre
212. Louvre
213. Three Ring Louvre Top
214. Louvre Top with Spigot
215. Louvre Top with Socket
216. Capped Louvre Top

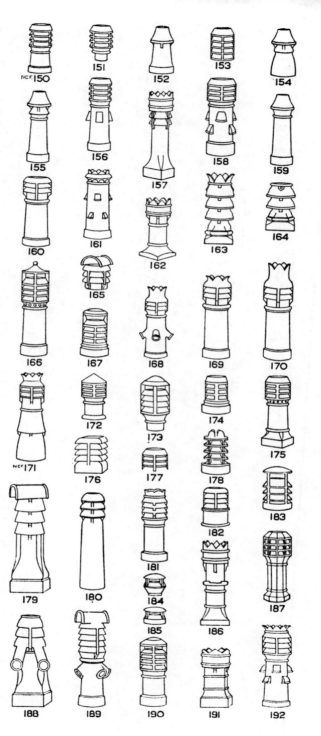

NCF 150 151 152 153 154
155 156 157 158 159
160 161 162 163 164
166 165 167 168 169 170
NCF 171 172 173 174 175
176 177 178 183
179 180 181 182 184 185 186 187
188 189 190 191 192

99

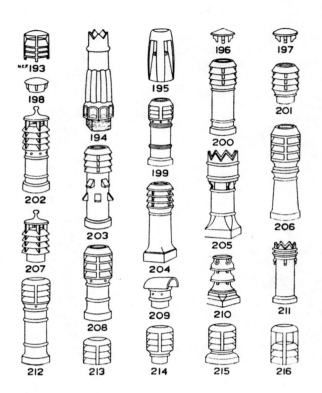

REF 193

198

194

195

196

197

201

202

199

200

206

203

207

204

205

211

212

208

209

210

213

214

215

216

Section 4
PLAIN   AND   ORNAMENTAL   SQUARE POTS

225. Plain Square	253. Plain Taper
226. Square Taper	254. Moulded Spike Top
227. Plain Taper	255-256. Moulded
228. Ribbed Taper	257. Fluted
229. Hooded Pocket	258. Plain Square
230. Square Panelled	259-260. Moulded
231. Plain Spiked	261. Ornamental Square
232. Fluted Spiked	262. Square Flue Lining
233. Plain Barrel Top	263. Plain Square
234. Plain Taper Pot.	264. Fluted Square
235. Plain Spiked Top	265. Square Panelled
236. Panelled Spike Top	266. Plain
237. Pocket Barrel Top	267-268. Ornamental Square
238. Panelled Spike	269. Plain Square
239. Plain Spike	270-271. Square Panelled
240. Beaded Plain	272. Ornamental Square
241. Panelled Spike	273. Ornamental Spiked
242. Ornamental Square	274. Hooded Square
243. Square Panelled	275. Plain Spiked
244. Panelled	276. Plain Square
245. Plain Square	277. Plain Square Spiked
246. Beaded Taper	278. Square Panelled
247. Plain Square	279. Square Spiked Panelled
248. Spike Panelled	280. Plain Square
249. Spike Plain	281. Square Spiked
250. Ornamental Panel	282. Plain Square
251. Plain Spike	283. Square Spiked Panelled
252. Moulded Square	284. Square Panelled

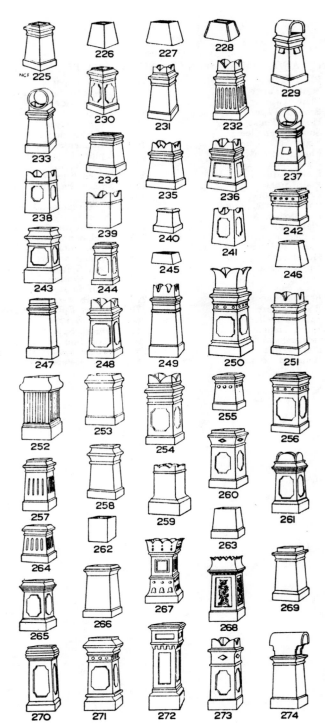

NCF 225 226 227 228 229 230 231 232 233 234 235 236 237 238 239 240 241 242 243 244 245 246 247 248 249 250 251 252 253 254 255 256 257 258 259 260 261 262 263 264 265 266 267 268 269 270 271 272 273 274

102

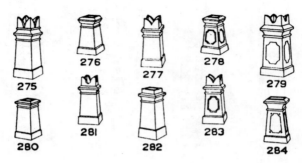

275   276   277   278   279   280   281   282   283   284

Section 5

PLAIN AND ORNAMENTAL OCTAGONAL POTS

300-322. Octagonal Pots in wide variety of design, heights and base sizes
323. Fluted Octagonal
324-325. Octagonal
326. Ornamental Octagonal
327-329. Octagonal
330-332. Ornamental Octagonal
333. Plain Octagonal
334, 335. Ornamental Octagonal
336. Hooded Octagonal
337. Ornamental Octagonal
338-340. Octagonal
341. Square Base Octagonal
342. Octagonal
343. Square Base Octagonal
344. Octagonal
345. Square Base Octagonal
346. Octagonal
347. Ornamental Octagonal
348. Octagonal
349-353. Ornamental Octagonal

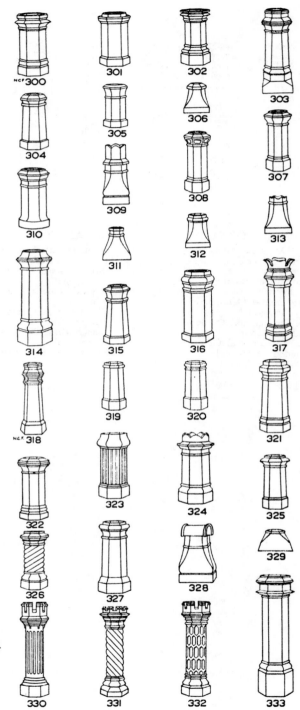

NCF300

301

302

303

304

305

306

307

310

309

308

313

311

312

314

315

316

317

NCF318

319

320

321

322

323

324

325

326

327

328

329

330

331

332

333

104

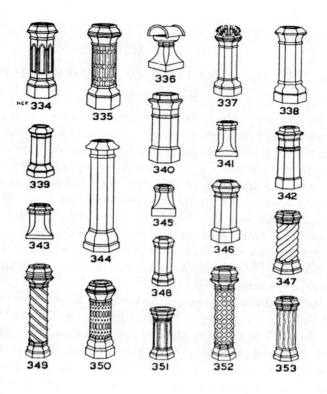

334 335 336 337 338
339 340 341 342
343 344 345 346
347 348
349 350 351 352 353

APPENDIX II

ON THE MANUFACTURE OF MEDIEVAL POTS
by Hugh E. Allen

The clay with which they were made obviously presented the potter with problems of shrinkage either in the drying out or at the stage of biscuit firing. Holes or incisions made in the pots enabled the thick clay to dry out at a more even rate. The actual composition of the clay can be decisive. A clay which is ungrogged is much more likely to crack from uneven shrinkage than is a clay which has been 'opened' with grog or sand. Chimney pots which have been excavated in the Chichester area have had amounts of flint added to their composition. Those found in Lewes and the east end of Sussex contain some sand.

Much of the ware produced by medieval kilns (an example of which was excavated in Orchard Street, Chichester, 1967) was glazed. The common glaze of that period was the galena glaze. The modern method of dipping a biscuited pot into the glaze mixture held in suspension in water was not known. Galena glaze is basically made from lead sulphide. This was either mixed with water and brushed on as slip is, or was dusted on to the pots. In the latter case the lead sulphide was in a dry powdered form. The galena glaze will fire to maturation in the biscuit firing. The resultant coating is of a yellow or buff colouring. Addition of copper either in the oxide form or some other compounded form, will vary the glaze from yellow to a quite dark green. Very few glazed pots have been excavated.

The completed pots were in the region of ten to thirteen inches tall. There are examples of pots up to fifteen inches. The bases of these are anything from six to eleven inches, and the tops from four to five inches. Most of the pots were made with a 'belly'. 'Long Farehams', the more recent hand-thrown pots, were nearly always thrown with this belly. The curves create an airflow that draws up the smoke. The holes usually made in the medieval pot were also probably intended to help the updraft.

Wrecclesham and Fareham Potteries

Just fifty years before chimney pots began to be considered as essential, the Fareham pottery opened. It was founded by the Harris family, who have since migrated across the country. Some members restarted their work in Dorset. As the plastic era came, other fields of work had to be found. The other part of the Harris family moved up to Wrecclesham near Farnham where they still live and work. After this migration (in 1873), the Sandy family took up the Fareham works. Both families produce very similar work. In the case of Sandy's pottery one has to rely upon the old potters who worked there for an idea of how it was run, since it has now been demolished.

The clay used for making the wares at Fareham was all dug locally. The quality was very good. After being dug it has to be cleaned of all loam and other organic impurities. It then becomes extremely plastic and strong after firing. Three very distinct layers of clay run across Fareham. The most important is the bottom strata—the blue clay. This seam runs under the Solent and can often be picked up in clods on the foreshore. The strata is about twenty-five feet thick and is reached after digging through the first two layers. Blue clay is never used on its own as it causes firing difficulties. 'It is like firing explosives'. So it is mixed with amounts of the other two types of clay.

The chimney pot maker needed considerable skill, much of this being employed in joining the two sections of the pot. The average height for a chimney pot being three feet, it has to be thrown in two sections. Many pots have been ordered in other combinations of eighteen inches. Pots six feet tall were not unknown. The height of any vessel to be thrown would depend on the length of the potter's arm, up to twenty inches being the average height. Allowing for shrinkage, the fired pot would be about eighteen inches high.

The techniques of mixing, kneading, wedging, turning, firing, etc., are well-known, making repetition here unnecessary. Less is known of the attractive forms of decoration given to Fareham and Wrecclesham pots. A band of white slip, sometimes two or three, is applied to the top of the pots with a brush while the pot is revolved on the wheel head. The band is enhanced by such devices as making a wavy line through the slip with a stick. This type of decoration has been in use for at least 150 years. The old pot that was removed from Harting Manor House recently was dated 1800 and signed 'G. Harris'. (The Harris family ran the Fareham potteries at that time). Other types of decoration used at Fareham in-line solutions and dipping in a black manganese slip at the leather hard stage.

BIBLIOGRAPHY

Encyclopaedia Britannica, art. *Chimney.*

Rumford, Count : *Fireplaces, Chimney-Stacks, and Flues.*

Wordsworth, W : *Guide to the Lake District.*

Dunning, G. C.: article 'Mediaeval Chimney-Pots' apud *Studies in Building History,* ed. E. M. Jope.

Dunning, G. C.: pamphlet, 'The Nottingham Louvre'.

Salzmann, L. F.: *Building in England down to* 1540 O.U.P.

Salzmann, L. F.: *English Industries of the Middle Ages.*

Lloyd, Nathaniel : *History of the English House.*

Addy and Summerson : *The Evolution of the English House.*

Marchant, E. W.: *Domestic Flues.* National Clayware Federation, 1966.

Wood, Margaret : *The English Mediaeval House;* Phoenix House, 1965.

Henderson, M.: *The Family House in England;* Phoenix House, 1964.

Gauger, M.: *Fires Improved,* 1713 : trans. into English, 1715.

Kelsall, M. R. and Harris, S.: *A Future for the Past,* Oliver & Boyd, 1961.

Clifton Taylor, A.: *The Pattern of English Building;* Batsford, 1962.

Jordan, R. P.: *A Picture History of the English House;* Hulton, 1959.

Davey, N.: *A History of Building Materials;* Phoenix House, 1961.

Barley, M. W.: *The House and Home;* Vista Books, 1963.

Barley, M. W.: *The English Farmhouse and Cottage;* Routledge & Kegan Paul, 1961.

Barry, R.: *The Construction of Buildings, Vol I;* Crosby Lockwood, 1962.

Stevenson, H. and L.: *Exterior Design;* Studio Books, London, 1963.

Summerson, J.: *Architecture in Britain,* 1530-1830 (Pelican History of Art).

Braun, H.: *Old English Houses;* Faber, 1962.

Ancient Reliques, London, 1813.

Blomfield, R.: *A Short History of Renaissance Architecture in England;* Bell, 1923.

Eberlein and Hubbard; *Historic Houses of the Hudson Valley;* Bonanza Books, 1942.

Howells, J. M.: *The Architectural Heritage of the Piscataqua;* Architectural Book Publishing Co. Inc., 1965.

Cruden, S.: *The Scottish Castle;* Nelson, 1960.

Dunbar, J. G.: *The Historic Architecture of Scotland;* Batsford, 1966.

A History of Art; Thames and Hudson, 1962.

McKay, W. B.: *Building Construction;* Longmans, 1955.

Hiort, J. W.: *A Practical Treatise on the Construction of Chimneys;* London, 1826.

Richardson, A. E., and Eberlein, H. D.: *The Smaller English House of the Later Renaissance;* Batsford, 1925.

Lloyd, N.: *Building Craftsmanship;* C.U.P.

Marks, Percy L.: *Chimneys and Flues;* Technical Press, London, 1935.

Paulsson, T.: *Scandinavian Architecture;* London, Leonard Hill, 1958.

Wright, Laurence; *Home Fires Burning;* Routledge & Kegan Paul, 1964.

INDEX

of proper-names

H

114